£8

AN ILLUMINATED CHRONICLE

Some Light on the Dark Ages of
Saint Milburga's Lifetime

THE SOUTH WEST VIEW OF WENLOCK ABBY, IN THE COUNTY OF SALOP.

The South West View of Wenlock Abbey [sic] . . . Samuel and Nathanial Buck, 1731

AN ILLUMINATED CHRONICLE

Some Light on the Dark Ages of Saint Milburga's Lifetime

by

Mary Gifford Brown

Bath University Press
1990

ISBN 0 86197 108 6

Printed by Redwood Press Limited,
Melksham, Wiltshire

Published by Bath University Press,
Claverton Down,
Bath BA2 7AY

Contents

Introduction

by The Right Honourable Lord Fletcher of Islington

'An Illuminated Chronicle' is the study of the monastic foundation at Much Wenlock and the life of Saint Milburga its founder. It deals with an aspect of the conversion period and the early days of Christianity in England which has hitherto been neglected by historians. This may be partly due to Bede's little knowledge or interest in Mercian affairs. Be that as it may, Mary Gifford Brown in her book has thrown valuable light on the significance of the part played by the kings of Mercia in the seventh and eighth centuries. She has pinpointed the prominent part played by women, many of whom were of royal blood, in the coversion period when the English peoples owed so much to the monastic order. Daughters of royal families were encouraged to become abbesses and thereby made their valuable contribution to the Christian education of England. 'An Illuminated Chronicle' highlights the life and work of one such family and in particular that of the princess-abbess Milburga.

Mary Gifford Brown has drawn her valuable information and observations from a wide selection of books and from the original latin text of the 'Vita Milburga' by Goscelin of Canterbury. The unique transcription of this text, part of a London University thesis written by Ms Angela Edwards in 1961 has been translated into modern English by Mr Keith Workman of Repton. It is a work of particular importance and the pivot of Mary Gifford Brown's illuminating study of Milburga's lifetime. I referred to Ms Edward's thesis on Goscelin's text and to Professor Finberg's book on 'The Early Charters of the West Midlands', in a paper I wrote for the British Archaeological Association in 1965 on 'The Pre-Conquest Churches at Much Wenlock'. These references drew Mary Gifford Brown's attention to the remarkable life story of the foundress of Much Wenlock Abbey. She recognised the need to place Milburga's name among the already known women ecclesiastical leaders of the day, notably Hilda of Whitby, Hildelith of Barking, Sexburga of Ely, Lioba of Bischofshein and others.

The 'Dark Ages' have long been bedevilled and neglected but the time is emerging in which students of history, and others, are beginning to realise their importance and significance. Much about them remains as cloudy as ever but thanks to present day research and to writings such as 'An Illuminated Chronicle', some light is being shed on the Anglo-Saxon period, and students are increasingly turning their attention to hitherto obscure facts.

My own interest in Anglo-Saxon Archaeology has spread over half a century. When I think of those early days when I started my studies, I recall a visit some sixty years ago to Sompting church near Worthing, Sussex. The local guide alleged the building to be Saxon but was unable to give any distinctive evidence for this view. This prompted me to study the essential characteristics of architecture between the Romans and the Normans, a period whose obtruse origins had hitherto escaped close scrutiny. I believed then that the method of using 'Long and Short' quoins to be the touchstone of Saxon building as distinct from Norman building. In 1944 I wrote the first of a series of papers for the British Archaeological Association, 'Long and Short Quoins and Pilaster Strips in Saxon Churches'. My research was inspired by the work of Professor Baldwin Brown, Sir Alfred Clapham, Professor Stenton and others who pioneered the Anglo Saxon studies in Britain. My friend Dudley Jackson contributed his invaluable technical ability. He was a skilled draftsman and builder and had an intuitive feeling for Anglo-Saxon architecture and a sympathetic understanding of the constructional problems which confronted those early builders in stone. I owed much to his genius for the observation of detail. His plans, drawings and photographs featured in each of the fifteen papers published by us between 1944 and 1968.

The examination of the structural features of Anglo-Saxon churches and the architectural techniques employed, led us on to study the history of several sites of that period. In 1962 after completing our research on the apse and nave at Wing, Buckinghamshire, we turned our attention to the surviving priory ruins at

Much Wenlock. The articles written by Rose Graham in 1939 and Dean Cranage in 1922 urged us to examine more closely the nature of the Pre-conquest buildings there. The need to reassess the origins of these monastic buildings was occasioned at that time by the publication in 1961 of transcriptions of important medieval manuscripts about Saint Milburga and Much Wenlock, by Professor Finberg. The appearance of this new historical material and appreciations led us, with the consent of the then owner, Mr Lewis Motley, and the Ministry of Works, to whose guardianship the site had been recently transferred, to conduct a series of excavations at the Priory in August 1963. Both the documentation of our findings and Professor Finberg's critical analysis form a valuable basis for this present study of the foundress and abbess of the Anglo-Saxon monastery that played an important role in the conversion to Christianity of the south west of England. Mary Gifford Brown succeeds in restoring the prominence that is due to Saint Milburga, which has been neglected for over twelve hundred years.

Acknowledgements

Grateful thanks are extended to:
    Lord Fletcher for his invaluable advice and direction.
    Keith Workman of Repton School for his translation of Goscelin of Canterbury's 'Vita Milburga'.
    Susan Youngs of the British Museum, Department of Medieval and Later Antiquities, for her valuable comments on the original text.
    Mark Cohen for his editorial advice.
    Mr Francis James Brown for listening to my many commentaries on the life and times of Saint Milburga.
    Columbia University Press, New York for permission to reprint the 'Description of a vision seen by a monk of the monastery at Wenlock'.
    The Royal Commission of Historical Manuscripts for the reproduction of the photograph of Much Wenlock Abbey today.
    The National Trust Photographic Library for the photograph of Long Mynd.
    The British Library for the reproduction of: the South West View of Wenlock Abbey, 1731; Wenlock Abbey, 1779, B. Meyer; the manuscripts of Goscelin's 'Vita Milburga'.

List of Illustrations

1   *Much Wenlock Abbey Today (1953)*

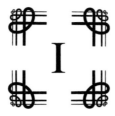

I

'Yet, though thus in rank but a priory, and subject to a rigid and extortionate control, Wenlock was the oldest and most priviledged, perhaps the wealthiest and most magnificent, of the religious houses of Shropshire.'   *The Reverend Eyton*

'Look around you and survey the fabric of creation. It is the work of an artist, of the Supreme Artist who has made all things beautiful in their season. He has gifted you too with a portion of His own nature and has formed you an artist, and you are bound in service to Him to exercise your creative gift and make the most of your affinity with what is beautiful. In the name of religion take up the brush and tongs and mallet, and spare not the cost or labour till the House of God that you build and adorn shall shine like the very fields of Paradise.'
Theophilus

'Spirit of Beauty, that dost consecrate
  With thine own hues all thou dost shine upon
  Of human thought or form, – where art thou gone?
Why dost thou pass away and leave our state,
This dim vast vale of tears, vacant and desolate?
  Ask why the sunlight not for ever
  Weaves rainbows o'er yon mountain-river,
Why aught should fail and fade that once is shown,
  Why fear and dream and death and birth
  Cast on the daylight of this earth
  Such gloom, – why man has such scope
For love and hate, despondency and hope?'
Percy Bysshe Shelley

1

Above close cropped lawns and neat gravel paths tower the remains of Much Wenlock Abbey, a beautiful specimen of Norman and Gothic architecture. The grace and grandeur of the surviving ruins still convey an impression of the wealth and importance held by this monastic house for a period of over nine centuries. During those years the walls of the monastery, the Priory church and the church of Holy Trinity rose and fell under the power of 'love and hate, despondency and hope.'

First founded by Merewald, king of that region called the Magonsaetan and presided over by his daughter Milburga until 720, the monastery flourished until the Danes ravaged and conquered Mercia in 874. It is generally accepted that monastic life at Much Wenlock ceased during the tenth century but a land charter dated 901 refers to land granted to the community of the church there. So it may be concluded that a remnant of monks of the early community kept the light of Christianity still burning albeit from a small candle flame.

The second foundation of Much Wenlock was a Minster built in 1050 by Leofric, the powerful Earl of Mercia who dedicated the church to the memory of Saint Milburga. Leofric was a friend of Edward the Confessor and became more famous for his wife Lady Godiva. He was a religious man and a generous one. The Minster at Much Wenlock was furnished and ornamented in the same lavish style as the several religious houses he founded during his lifetime. It is recorded in the Domesday book that the status of his new and handsome church was changed by Earl Roger of Salop when he made it an Abbey. Earl Roger had been brought over to England in 1067 by William the Conqueror who duly enriched him with the earldom of Shropshire. He was an influential man and a benefactor of the famous monastery of Cluny in France. When Earl Roger found that monks were needed to serve the church and monastery of Saint Milburga he asked for Cluniac monks to be sent over from France. They came from Sainte Marie of La Charité, a subsidary monastery of Cluny. This foreign visitation to the quiet valley, under the shadow of Wenlock Edge, lasted until the dissolution of the monastery in the sixteenth century and the spread of the Cluniac Order to Saint Milburga's religious house held fast for over four centuries, through political upheavals, famine, pestlilence and persecution.

It is quite likely that there were feelings of hostility towards these religious strangers who invaded the rural community of Much Wenlock. Perhaps they ousted the monks already installed there and commandeered the memory of their relatively unknown Saint. But early in the twelfth century a 'miracle' occurred that changed the role of these French monks and altered their prestige. When the bones of their much loved Saint Milburga were discoverd by accident they became the honoured custodians of precious, wonder-working relics. The full story of this chance occurance and of the miracles brought about by the relics was written down by Odo of Ostia in his 'Odo's Invention', in 1101. The account has been transposed from the Latin text. (Jackson and Fletcher):-

'The monks brought over by Earl Roger had acquired, possibly as one of the costly ornaments with which Leofric had endowed his church, a silver casket reputed to contain the remains of Saint Milburga. The brethren decided to open the casket to verify this belief. They did so. The shrine was empty. Not long afterwards, one of the lay brothers, Raymond by name, in the church of the Holy Trinity which is about a stone's throw from the oratory of Saint Milburga, was doing some renewal and repair work to parts of the building over the altar that had fallen into disrepair. He noticed among other things an old box jutting out above the altar. Inside the box was a very old document written in Old English by a priest, Alstan. This stated that the body of Saint Milburga was buried in the church near the altar. But a long time had passed since that altar had been above the ground. It had either disintegrated through the passage of time, or been destroyed during the desolation of the region. The monks obtained permission,

3

indeed direction, of Anselm, Archbishop of Canterbury, to excavate and find the burial. But the actual discovery was inadvertent. On the vigil of Saint John the Baptist, while the monks were celebrating the night office, an event occurred in the monastery of the Holy Trinity in the very place where the document said the holy body lay. Two boys were playing when the ground under their feet collapsed, and they sank up to their knees into a kind of circular pit. At the sight of this, Raymond, the lay-brother, ran off to the monastery of Saint Milburga where the brethren were singing matins. As it was night, nothing was done until morning. Then, with tools, the ground was excavated and the bones of the Saint exposed, together with remains of iron bands. The sacred limbs had been buried in a wooden coffin. No signs of the altar mentioned in the parchment had yet appeared. On the following day the brethren began to dig throughout the whole church. Eventually there appeared beyond any possible doubt the foundations of the altar mentioned in the document, near to which, as was universally known, the holy body had been found the previous day. The brethren washed the bones and relaid them in that same shrine. Later they washed them again and enclosed them in a new shrine. They remained upon the altar of that same church, until the day of their translation, that is the feast of the Purification of the Blessed Virgin Mary.'

With the sacred relics in their possession the Cluniac monks took over the cult of Saint Milburga and their own institution took root and flourished in the religious house of the Anglo-Saxon princess. Finally in the sixteenth century her bones were burned in the market square of Much Wenlock in front of the whole community gathered there as a demonstration against hagiolatry.

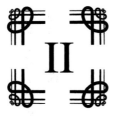

II

My God, I heard this day
That none doth build a stately habitation
  But he that means to dwell herein.
  What house more stately hath there been,
Or can be, than is Man? to whose creation
  All things are in decay.

George Herbert

'Before considering the beginnings of convent life as the work
of women whose existence rests on a firm historic basis, we
must enquire into the nature of women-saints. From the earliest times of established Christianity the lives of men and
women who were credited with special holiness have formed a
favorite theme of religious narratives, which were intended to
keep their memory green and to impress the devout with
thoughts of their saintliness.' *Lisa E. Eckenstein*

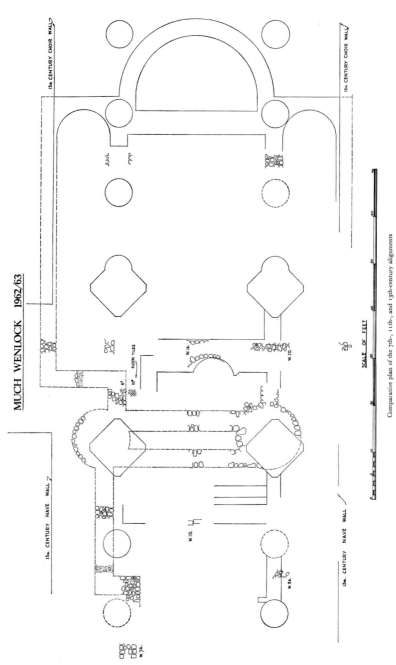

2 *Comparative plan of the 7th-, 11th-, and 13th-century alignments*

3   Trench Line 1/1 (extension), wall 1A

4   *Trench Line 8/8, wall 8A*

The bright flames of that sixteenth century bonfire give us our first light on the person and character of the foundress of Much Wenlock Abbey. They were kindled to destroy every trace of a woman whose life had been remarkable and whose influence had been so strong and lasting that she had become worshipped as a saint. The strength of the sentiment held for the memory of Saint Milburga was built into the stonework that grew up around and over the foundations of her original monastery. Archaeologists in the twentieth century have contributed detailed and authoritative accounts of some of these buildings. (Cranage, 1922; Graham, 1939; Jackson and Fletcher, 1965; Woods, 1987; Cox and Watson, 1987). They have unravelled the compexity of the architecture and have given a chronological order to the construction of the monastery. It was necessary for Cranage, Jackson and Fletcher and more recently H. Woods, to open up trenches in order to expose the wall courses belonging to the Anglo-Saxon period. Those walls appeared to be founded two feet 6 ins. below the level of the present day turf. The greater part of the ruins of the original monastery lie hidden beneath the surface and little remains to give much indication of its size and extent. Within the confines of the Priory church and the church of Holy Trinity the seventh century walls have been superimposed by later building but there is enough evidence from the surviving fabric to reinforce the view that –:

'in Milburga's time there were at least two churches of her monastic community (apart from her Oratory, and perhaps other oratories), one on the priory site and one on the site of the Holy Trinity. It is now reasonably clear that one of these – on the priory site – was for the use of the monks, and the other – on the site of Holy Trinity – for the nuns, and that Milburga was buried in the nuns' church – on the site of Holy Trinity, parts of which still survive.'   *Jackson and Fletcher*

The archaeological findings and architectural measurements of the 'stately habitation' of Much Wenlock Abbey do not contribute any direct knowledge of the character or the way of life of Saint Milburga. All traces of her community have sadly disappeared and so far no buriel ground has been uncovered that might give us even a clue as to how many monks and nuns were living there during her life time. The mud walls that provided their living quarters were washed away long ago by the rain laden years. In other parts of the country recent archaeological activities, field walking, aerial survey and the study of cemeteries and settlements has brought new light to bear on early Anglo Saxon life. The close analysis of artifacts found with human remains, the study of how graves were grouped and given certain features of importance, and the examination of how cemeteries related to Anglo Saxon settlements and other archaeological or historical data give more knowledge than has ever hitherto been known. Recent excavations of Anglo-Saxon churches and monasteries such as Whitby and Deerhurst have revealed a much clearer picture of the size and lay-out of those early ecclesiastical centres. Leslie Webster writes of this modern knowledge:

'But virtually nothing was known (before the 1940s) about how the Anglo-Saxons lived: their houses, their diet, their life-expectancy, their illnesses, their social composition how they used the land, what crops they grew, what animals they reared; how crafts were organised, how goods were distributed, how and when towns came about; what their monasteries looked like, how their churches were used; what had happened to the Romano-British population, – the list could go on almost indefinitely. Of course, the answers to some of these questions remain almost as obscure today; it would be over-bold to claim that archaeology is going to solve every query, but it is encouraging to look back on the work of the last forty years and see how radically our understanding of Anglo-Saxon England has been altered by the new directions archaeology has taken in this period.'   *L. Webster*

Here and there among the vast number of Anglo-Saxon sites being examined today we may get a clearer picture of life as it was during the seventh and eighth centuries. Where it is appropriate, comparisons can be drawn between Much Wenlock and other rural communities at that time and between Milburga's double monastery and similar religious houses of that date. By this process of examining a much wider picture of Anglo-Saxon England some of our queries can be solved about the life of the ruling class from which Milburga was drawn and how the property and people were managed under their care. Archaeologists and historians have produced maps and detailed accounts of the climate of England during that period and the spread of forest and arable land. They have been able to give us a broad indication of the lines of communication between one part of the country and another, the use of rivers and roads. Maps and diagrams show the concentration of the population, the scatter of villages and towns. (Hill, 1981; Finberg, 1972). Kate Pretty's thesis on The Settlement of the Severn and Avon Valleys in the Fifth and Sixth centuries AD., gives an excellent background to an examination of the Magonsaetan where Milburga's father ruled and over which her double monastery presided.

The results of archaeological research give us glimpses of Anglo-Saxon life as it might have been held in common to a generation that spanned Milburga's life time, 664–720. It is possible to equate Milburga's circumstances with those known to be similar, to get some idea of what diet she enjoyed, what crops grew on her land, the shape and structure of her housing, what utensils she used, clothes and furnishings and how these were made, the illnesses and hardships of climate she might have endured, her modes of transport and the important places she might have visited. But in order to draw closer to discovering the unique nature of this early woman-saint we must turn to literary evidence.

In 1961 Leicester University Press published H. P. R. Finberg's translations of the Early Charters of the West Midlands. In his Introduction Finberg writes: 'The Latin and vernacular charters of the Old English period are the documentary foundations of English local history. They are also a source of primary value for the national historian.' The writs, wills and memoranda relating to land transactions throughout four shires, including Shropshire, are presented in chronological order from the seventh century to the Norman Conquest. Such a painstaking task of compiling a 'hand-list' of charters, involved a close scrutiny of documents that were often hard to come by and whose original text was either in Anglo-Saxon or in Latin styled by colloquial usage. Finberg's work of translating the charters relating to Milburga and her monastery at Much Wenlock has opened the lens wider through which we can penetrate the intervening twelve and a half centuries. Though the picture we see is blurred by the passage of time and lack of evidence, much can be learned from the background to these charters, the signatures that accompany them and the dates of the transactions. These names and events weave a pattern against which the story of Milburga's life stands out in relief.

Further to the Shropshire charters Finberg made a reappraisal of early manuscripts of extreme importance, the so-called Testament of Milburga which he published in translation for the first time. In his Introduction Finberg writes that this document 'incorporates passages which show every sign of having been transcribed verbatim from five authentic ancient charters. It is itself a narrative which throws new light on the history of Milburga's foundation at Much Wenlock. This autobiographical statement, was professedly drawn up or dictated by Milburga herself towards the close of her life'. It was incorporated in the 'Life of St. Milburga' written by Goscelin, 1101–1105, a leading professional hagiographer in the twelfth century. Goscelin came over to England from France and spent many years travelling from monastery to monastery. He searched their archives and no doubt listened to stories handed down by word of mouth, to compile his biographies of the founders of these monasteries or their patron saints. Almost as frustrating as trying to focus on a clear profile of Saint Milburga from these early writings has been my attempt to trace the present day whereabouts of Ms A. J. M. Edwards who in 1960 wrote her M.A. thesis on 'Odo of Ostia's History of the Translation of St. Milburga and its Connection with the Early History of Much Wenlock Abbey'. Ms Edwards drew much of her information of the early history of Milburga and her monastery from Goscelin's 'Life of Saint Milburga'. In her thesis she includes a full transcription of the text of this 'Vita' from the Lincoln Cathedral Chapter Manuscript. Thanks to her transcription and the translation of it into English by Keith Workman, Milburga's genealogy and several stories relating to her life, as well as her 'Testament', have been made available for this study and to provide 'religious narratives to keep her memory green'.

A year or so before Milburga entered the monastery at Much Wenlock Bede, then a small boy of seven, began his education in the monastery of Wearmouth in County Durham, under Abbot Benedict Biscop. Bede continued to live in the north of England as an ordinary monk for the rest of his life devoting his time to studying and writing. In 731, several years after the death of Milburga he completed his 'Ecclesiastical History of the English People'. Henry Mayr-Harting describes this great literary work as fundamental to the knowledge of early Anglo-Saxon history. He writes, 'The Ecclesiastical History is like one of the great dark-age brooches; it combines a certain grandeur and sweep of overall design with the utmost delicacy of detail'. Bede gathered the material for his writing from the monastery library and from monks with whom he was in correspondence and the scope of his knowledge of historical events was limited to the ecclesiastical centres he considered to be of greatest prominence. He hardly travelled at all and it is recorded that he visited only York and Lindisfarne. This may be a primary reason why he gave no mention of Milburga or of her prestigious religious house. Bede seems to have shown little interest in the growth of Christianity in the west and southwest of England and only vaguely refers to the Westerners of the Hereford – Shropshire area as 'those people who dwell beyond the River Severn'. However the 'Ecclesiastical History' unfolds much of the story of the conversion of the Anglo-Saxons and its chapters provide a great deal of background knowledge for this study. It is at the momentous event of the conversion of the Anglo-Saxons of the Magonsaetan in the west of England that the story of Saint Milburga begins.

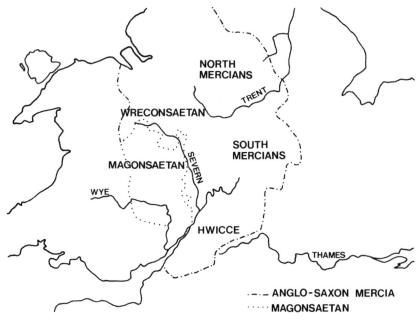

5   *The Mercian Kingdom in the 7th century*

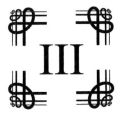

III

'655. In this year Penda perished and the Mercians became Christians. (654) In this year Oswiu killed Penda at Winwaedfeld, and 30 princes with him, and some of them were kings.....And Peada, the son of Penda succeeded to the kingdom of the Mercians.'   *Anglo-Saxon Chronicle*

'The Holy Grail'
... And in the strength of this I rode,
   Shattering all evil customs everywhere,
   And past thro' Pagan realms, and made them mine,
   And clash'd with Pagan hordes, and bore them down,
   And broke thro' all, and in the strength of this
   Come victor.'   *Alfred, Lord Tennyson*

'The Victory (of Winwaed) was a great event in the history of English Christianity. It marked the end of the heathen power, and since the death of Penda no secular ruler has openly identified himself with an anti-Christian policy in this country.'   *C. J. Godfrey*

In the middle of the seventh century the kingdom of Mercia occupied a great part of England. It stretched from the lower Trent in the north east, through the Midlands to the river Severn and the borders of Wales in the west. Mercia was ruled by the pagan king Penda, 'the most formidable king of England' (Stenton) Penda subjugated a diversity of peoples and a number of smaller kingdoms but his power was never safe for long. He had to travel vast distances with his army to make new conquests and to defend his Mercian boundaries. By the year 655 Penda's chief enemy was the Christian king Oswiu, ruler of Bernicia, a division of the kingdom of Northumbria. The two kings had been linked by the marriage of their two children, Oswiu's elder son was married to a daughter of Penda. But they struggled for power over the kingdom of Deira, a division of Northumbria. In 655 Penda decided to put an end to his rival; he marched northwards with his army, strengthened by thirty Welsh allies and their troops. The battle took place in the country close to Leeds which was flooded at the time by the swollen river Winwaed. Oswiu despaired that the odds were against him as he faced the 'Pagan hordes'. He tried to buy peace by offering gifts to Penda and finally 'made a deal' with God that He should give him victory if he offered his baby daughter for a lifetime's service to the Church. Whatever power guided the hand of Destiny that day the outcome was victory for Oswiu who then in turn became 'the greatest of the English kings'. (*Godfrey*)

The heir to the kingship of Mercia was Penda's son Peada who had already joined the ranks of the Christians before his father's death. He had travelled to Northumbria to ask the hand of Oswiu's daughter Alhflaed and the union was granted on condition that he accepted baptism. So Peada returned home to Mercia with his new bride and his newly found faith, accompanied by four priests who would help him towards spreading Christianity. The old pagan king tolerated the conversion of his son; he had not long to live.

After Penda's defeat and death at Winwaed the victorious Oswiu decided to install Peada as Overlord of the Middle-Angles of Mercia, in 655. This reign lasted only a few years. Peada was treacherously murdered and his brother Wulfhere succeeded him. He too was a devout Christian and he continued to further the success of the Church throughout the Midlands.

Mercia was divided into provinces, ruled by under-kings who were possibly blood relatives of the great Mercian dynasty. One such province was the Magonsaetan, a district stretching across the plain of Herefordshire north of the Wye, and over the hills and valleys of what is now Shropshire. In 655 the Magonsaetan was ruled by Merewald the future father of Milburga he was at that date about thirty years of age and still a pagan. But the gateway to Christianity had been opened and a steady flow of monks from the Celtic Northumbrian Church were pentrating this furthest west territory of the kingdom, bringing with them a new message of Light and Hope for this life and the life to come. Merewald was soon to become a convert to this new Faith.

Wenlock Abbey, Shropshire

Publish'd Oct. 16, 1779, by V. Green, Mezzotinto Engraver to his Majesty, and to the Elector Palatine, N°29 Newman Street, Oxford Street.

6   *Wenlock Abbey, 1779, drawn by B. Mayer*

IV

The story of Merewald's conversion is told in legendary style in Goscelin's 'Life of Saint Milburga'. It has the flavour of an Old Testament story and as such it deserves to be included in full and because it bears direct relationship to the events that follow in Milburga's life.

'What I am now telling I have learnt partly by reading and partly by conversation with a certain old venerable priest. He said King Merewald of the Mercians was devoted to Paganism when the holy priest Edfrid, a man famous for his learning and renowned for his life, came to convert from the regions of Northumbria, warned by a heavenly message. As it is said, he undertook himself this divine message to proceed to the land of the Mercians to a place called Readesmith and to preach there the word of God, to convert the King and his people who were pagans to Christianity. St. Edfrid set off therefore and started the task of preaching, not knowing the King and the district to where he had been ordered by heaven to proceed. From heaven the way was told to him, and from heaven he was led right to the place.

Finally therefore he reached the place at sunset. Day was covered in night and the new visitor lacking shelter was protected in the open air during the night. Lest however he might be despondent from the uncertain reason for his journey he is visited by divine power fortelling the king's conversion. For while he was sitting at a small meal in the evening, having first paid to God due praises and prayers, a huge lion approached, with his mane bristling over his shoulders. When he saw the lion the holy man like an intrepid Godfearer by no means gave

19

way, but as if to someone sent from heaven handed to him a crust from his bread. The beast took this morsel handed to him, no longer like a lion but more gently than a lamb with a bland mouth, and rolling on the ground before the feet of the provider as he calmly ate it. What more? The lion having fed disappeared and the holy man spent the night in the place.

The sun returned to the upper sky, the day shone forth golden bright. The visitor having prayed, arose from the place and went around the neighbourhood and found out where the king and his family lived for whom he was looking. A house was picked for him to be guest in and he was looked after by one of the king's soldiers.'

'The following night the king had a dream and when he told it in the morning to his court none of his court could interpret it. The soldier was reminded about his guest that he had taken in, and as the Pharoah had been advised by his visiar about Joseph as an interpreter of his dream he suggested to the king, "My Lord the king", he said, "your excellency should bid that a certain man be presented whom last night I received under my roof as a guest. His manners seem different from ours and if I am not mistaken he is a disciple of the Christian faith. For he denounces our Gods and reviles them and promises and threatens our worship of them will bring the punishment of everlasting death. Perhaps if he hears the dream of my lord the king he will be, I fancy, no false interpreter of it." The king said to the soldier, "Let such your guest be summoned quickly."

'When the Christian ambassador had been summoned into the presence of the king, the king thus began to tell him his dream.

"While the past night held me sunk in sleep on my couch I seemed to see two foul and huge dogs tearing me by the throat. Then from the country a certain character of venerable countenance, with his hair shorn round his ears into a crown of locks, came to my assistance. He rescued me from the fangs of the dogs powerfully with a golden key which he carried in his hand. So it happens that the vast size of the dogs and their ravenous attack on me terrifies me, and thus I am comforted by my speedy rescue and the pleasing vision of my rescuer. But I do not know what omen such foul a vision holds, so wild and uncontrolled, or what means such a pleasant person my rescuer, so respectable a key bearer by whom my anxious mind is restored".

'The king had finished speaking and the disciple of Christ reponds. "You are to be congratulated on your dream, O King, for it tends to your eternal salvation. My King, listen and understand what good is portended by the so horrible appearance of those attacking you and striving to throttle you, and what is foretold by the so pleasant appearance of the key bearer, your liberator. The huge foul dogs are the attendants of darkest Pluto, the enemies of your life and mortal salvation, to whose jaws you will be given as prey and food, and being devoured you will always be devourable. In this way you will always be dying and never end by death your perpetual terrors, your sulphurous miasmas, gnashing of teeth, burning of fire, and vast and intolerable penalties when you are tortured by them in the middle of Hell. Unless, you renounce paganism completely and in your whole heart are converted to Christ, the son of the living God."

"You must revere that key bearer by whose power you are freed, just as it seemed you were freed from so wild and voracious beasts. He is the gatekeeper and chief of the heavenly kingdom and on earth the vicar of Christ the saviour of the world. For his golden key is the power of heaven by which whatsoever he binds is bound and whatsoever he frees is freed. To him you will build a house in your kingdom to offer praise and thanks, night and day, to the Superior King' believing in him in your heart and confessing him with your lips and putting on also the raiment of his baptism of the life of peace. You will abjure devilish rites and foreswear the profane worship of idolatry, so that you may deserve to be suitable for the abode of the King of heaven. In his kingdom is continual and blessed joy. It has no knowledge of failure and death and you will be its happy and everlasting inheritor when you are freed from the teeth of the dogs, through the taking up of the holy faith of Saint Peter, your liberator. Who by the confession of Christ the son of the living God earned the keys and the headship of Paradise".

'By these and various rudiments of faith, our holy hero preached Christ to the King and by his preaching tried to convert the King to Christ. When he had heard all this carefully, the King said to the interpreter of his salvation:

"Whatever your Christian learning teaches me I am prepared to undertake devoted subjection to it, so long as I am able to escape the jaws of so horrible a beast."

'Preceded therefore by clemency from on high, the king destroyed and abominated all his idols. He laid aside the badges of rule, his sceptre, purple and crown and he put on sackcloth and sprinkled his hair with ashes. He grieved and groaned and was wholly sunk in penintence. He fell at the feet of the Saint, he abjured paganism and professed the worship of God. He is reborn in the Holy water, he is more saintly a Christ-worshipper and a man of instant devotion to everthing his evangelist explained to him. The course of God's incarnation had now preceded $6 \times 20 + 6$ illustrations, when Merewald, King of the Mericans adopted from the holy priest Edfridd, the grace of Christian rebirth.'

After the conversion of the King, as recounted, which was foretold divinely by the man of God, a place for founding a house is chosen for the royal liberator, the doorman of the heavenly kingdom. Whence that place was later turned into the monastery. The house when founded was royally enriched, richly endowed with royal things and wealth. In charge of it was placed the blessed Edfridd. The King therefore, realising the evidence of truth, was so ardent in blaze of holiness that he seemed with the greatest ardour to restore in him whatever he had neglected in past times. What he had amassed for himself by wordly power, with the bowels of compassion he restored to Christ's poor. He founded and constructed for God churches all over, and when they were built he gave them rich farms and 'families'.'

Merewald was baptised in the year 660. Under his leadership Christianity spread fast among people whose loyalty and unquestioning willingness to work for their King characterised Anglo-Saxon society of that day. How long it took to evangelise the villages and remote settlements of the Magonsaetan is impossible to ascertain. The Christian message may have been familiar to some, where the Celtic missions were already established. The Celtic monks who came with Edfridd from Northumbria followed the tradition set down by Saint Columba of Iona and Aidan of Lindisfarne. They went about their work on foot rejecting any of the amenities that might separate them from the level of the people they were evangelising. They ate sparsely and slept rough and devoted themselves to a strenuous routine of prayer, penitence and study. Their knowledge and veneration of the Bible was reflected in all aspects of life even to the obeying of Old Testament food regulations. They preached a message of salvation and the promise of eternal life that brought the light of new hope to a pagan society living in the shadow of fate. These new converts understood that homage was no longer due to uncompassionate gods of thunder, war and fertility and that sacrifice to devils was no longer needed when the destiny of darkness gave way to the promise of redemption.

'By the middle of the seventh century it must have been clear that two distinct forms of the Christian religion were competing for the spiritual allegiance of the Anglo-Saxon peoples. There could have been no doubt by now of the ultimate triumph of Christianity itself. Heathenism, though it was to linger on in the life of the people for generations, was as a living force perceptibly waning.'   *Godfrey*

Side by side the Celtic and Roman missions worked for the conversion of England. In Kent the Roman church was firmly established where it had been founded by Augustine and his followers a century before. In other parts of the east, north east and Wessex, ecclesiastical centres were growing in number and importance. Wherever the Roman church was established its connections with the continent and its allegiance to the papacy became apparent and it brought to England the prestige of the civilisations of Gaul and Rome. Books and education, new arts and techniques of architecture and building were introduced to a degree that had not been known since the Romans themselves had conquered the British Islands six hundred years before. In contrast the Magonsaetan had few of these traditions and connections with the Frankish kingdoms and Rome. Trading routes to the Continent from the Welsh Border country were not nearly so easy and short as those that spanned across the English Channel, and those Welsh borders needed constant surveillance against warring princedoms. One is free to suppose that when Merewald embraced Christianity he would have seen the immense benefits that the new Faith might have for his kingdom and the far reaching effects from an affiliation with the church of Rome. Those benefits were to be provided by his new Christian bride.

It is not known whether Merewald celebrated his baptism into Christianity at the same time as he formalised his marriage to Domneva, daughter of the Kentish prince Eormenred. Domneva's first cousin had recently become the wife of Merewald's brother Wulfhere, Overlord of Mercia. With this second marriage Mercia was contracted to a powerful royal house that had benefited from Christian teaching and education for three generations. The marriage of Merewald to Domneva bears direct relevance to our story; Milburga was the daughter of that union.

After the preface to 'The Life of Saint Milburga' Goscelin launches into her genealogy and gives an account of 'the glorious stock of royal dignity' from which 'this star of gently nobility arose'.

'The famous King Aethelbert was the great great grandfather of the saintly virgin Milburga whom the first teacher of the Angles, St. Augustine, made the first worshipper of Christ among English Kings, to whose faith as the dawn precedes the day so he was preceded by the light of holiness, his wife, Bertha, daughter of the King of the Franks. For a Christian woman had married a pagan husband to whom she had shone forth like the dawn in the earth below. The kingdom which had existed like a black night under a profane King, the son of night, had been decorated as only she could by the Queen of the kingdom, the daughter of light, as if by the moon the mistress of night, by the discipline of the faith and the learning of her character.'

'. . . From them was bore Eadbald the most noble heir to the Kingdom, most devoted follower of his father's faith and most energetic builder of God's churches, with his sister Aethelburga, queen of Edwin King of Northumbria. She when widowed, losing husband and kingdom, returned to her aformentioned brother who was then King of Kent. She then led a monastic life and ended her days at Lyminge where she was buried in glory for her deserts. The aforementioned King of Kent married Emma, daughter of the Kings of Augustine Gaul. Their royal wedding produced royal flowers worthy of royal honour as heirs Eormenred, Eorcenberht, and Eanswith, a virgin worthy of heaven whose virginal dissertation at the convent at Folkestone fought worthily for God. Eorcenberht was chosen by his father as King (after the death of his father) and receiving the kingdom married Saint Sexburga the daughter of Anna and King Hereswith. Her sister was the famed Virgin Edeldritha, from whom God piously afforded his happy children, Kings Egbert and Latorius and queens Eorcengota and Eormenhild. The first of these, King Egbert, succeeded into his father's kingdom. His sister, the Virgin Eorcengota, set out abroad across the sea out of love of religion and died as a missionary. Eormenhild married Wulfhere, King of the Mercians from whom the virgin Werburg, blessed jewel of God, shone forth. Eormenred, famous by the happy omen of his name (for in English it means the comfort of the afflicted, in which name he was deservedly powerful through the attention to piety and duty rather than by command), by God's grace happily begot two imperial and martyr-like roses, Saints Aethelred and Aethelberht from his royal wife named Oslafa. On the death of these two who were brutally killed and fraudulently concealed, a light shining from the skies like a huge solar ray shining out above them, revealed the act to all. Many are not ignorant of the continuation of this story, which I for that reason pass over for the sake of brevity. The memorable Eormonred also had four daughters most deserving of praise, Domneva, Ermemberga, Ermembyrga and Ermengytha, who were the pearls, gleaming with the diverse rays of virtues as fitting the crown of the Eternal King; the Eternal King himself bound them to him. Of them Domneva the hope and glory of holy posterity was given in marriage to Merewald, King of the Magonsaetan in the western part of the Mercians. He shared the kingdom, born third and his brother Wulfhere born second, for they were brothers, the sons of Penda, most valliant King at whose death they had succeeded as twin rulers of their native kingdom. They had two whole brothers, one of them the first born and the other last born viz. Peada and Ethelred.'

Merewald had chosen well. His bride would bring him the prestige of a great aristocracy and the benefits of an allegiance with the powerful kingdom of Kent.

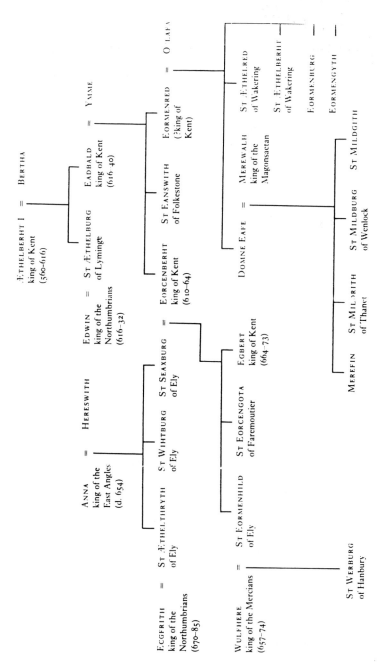

7 *Family Tree from King Ethelbert of Kent to Milburga of Wenlock*

27

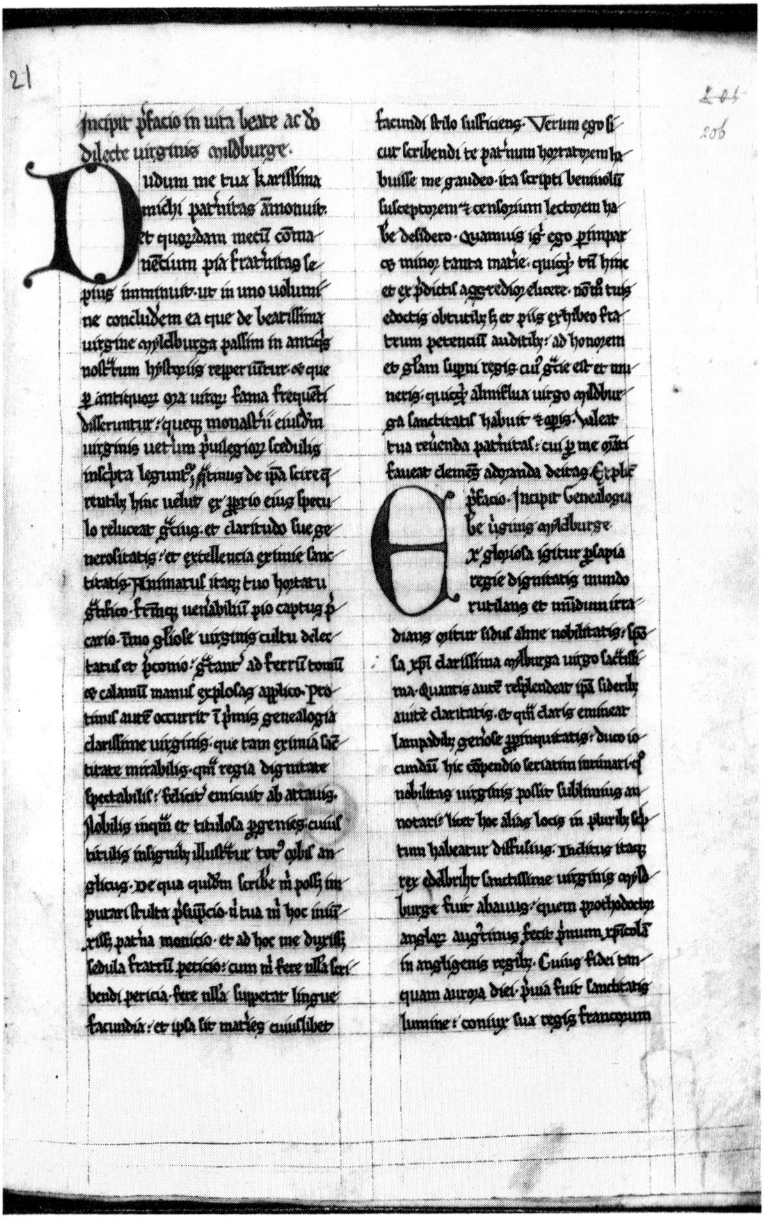

8 Goscelin: Vita Milburga, Mss. folio 206

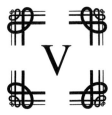

V

'A king must pay, when he obtains a queen, with cups and with rings. It is proper for both to be generous with gifts. The man of rank is to concentrate on battle, and the woman to thrive, loved by her people; to be cheerful, to preserve knowledge, to be open-hearted in the giving of horses and treasures. At the mead-pouring she will always before a great company first of all greet the ruler of princes with the first cup, present it to the lord's hand; and teach him wisdom for them both together living in that community.' *C. Fell*

'Much of the custom regulating matters like marriage and inheritance was handed on orally, and cannot all be recovered from the scattered references to these topics. It is in this province of the law that the acceptance of Christianity made most difference.' *D. Whitelock*

'... He took a wife, who the wise men of the kingdom say was of noble birth, well-grown, with fair hair, large-eyed, of fine shape, with queenly figure and strong limbs and well-made legs and the best of feet, and long fingers and thin nails; kindly and eloquent, and good at food and drink; wise and prudent, a woman of good counsel, merciful towards her kingdom, charitable to the needy, and just in all things...' *K. Jackson*

29

No heroic verse has survived to describe that particular noble event, the marriage of the first Christian rulers of the Magonsaetan, Merewald and Domneva; an event no doubt celebrated with singing, blessings and prayers and customary feasting and revelry. Glimpses of similar scenes have been preserved in 'Beowulf', the epic poem whose chance survival in manuscript has provided description of such royal celebrations. Here the King is surrounded by his noble warriors who feast with him and sleep 'when the benches were cleared away and pillows and bedding were spread upon the floor'. (Beowulf) The banquet lasted for days, there was heavy eating and drinking, the Queen herself fulfilling the role of 'cup bearer' to the King and his guests. 'This abundant confirmation of a single episode suggests that much of the incidental background of 'Beowulf' represents a genuine and accurate tradition.' (Stenton) In 'The Exeter Book', circa. 975, we read that 'One shall gladden men gathered together, delight those sitting on the benches at the beer where the joy of the drinkers is great. One shall sit at his lord's feet with his harp, receive treasure and ever swiftly sweep the strings, let the plectrum, which leaps, sound aloud the nail with its melody; great is the desire for him.' (Crossley-Holland) Such merry-making and entertainment were traditional to Anglo-Saxon life, welcome respites from the hardships of the daily round and the dangers of war.

What impression of Domneva can we intuit from this series of events? How well was she protected and prepared for the long journey that took her so far, both geographically and culturally from the safety and comforts of the Kentish royal house? Her great grandfather King Aethelbert had laid down laws defending women's rights, stipulating the financial aspects of marriage and making provision for widows. He dictated that the prospective husband should give a payment of money, a morgengifu or 'morning gift' to his chosen lady, money not paid to the family of the bride but to the woman herself. Once married the wife had a right to a share in the matrimonial estate and the matrimonial finances too were shared property. These laws drawn up under the influence of the Christian Roman Church gave recognition to woman's status and responsibility.

'Marriage agreements were drawn up between kin but this does not imply that the girl had no rights or say in the matter. It is fairly obvious that where substantial transactions were involved she would require the services of her older kin as legal and financial advisers. There is no indication that any direct profit accrued to the girl's family and no indication that her wishes were not considered.' *Fell*

Domneva was about seventeen years of age when she made her decision to become Merewald's wife. She was a young woman of substance, educated with all the refinements that Kentish links with the Frankish civilisation had offered. Moreover she had been nurtured in a Christian family with the love and discipline of Christian teaching. Domneva's decision to marry a convert and to assist with the spreading of the Gospel in unfamiliar territory was to carry on a tradition already established by some of her prominent female relatives of the Kentish royal family. Her Christian Great Grandmother Bertha had come over to England from France to marry the pagan King Aethelbert. With her priest, Liudhard, she had founded the church of Saint Martin outside Canterbury, therein to worship and to pray for the conversion of her husband. Queen Bertha had welcomed Saint Augustine and his priests to Kent when they were sent by Pope Gregory to evangelize England. Great must have been her joy when King Aethelbert accepted Baptism and the Christian Church became established in the kingdom. Bertha's daughter Ethelberga made another long journey to marry a pagan king. Together with her priest, Paulinus, she travelled to Northumbria to become the wife of King Edwin. Through her the message of the Gospels held fast in the North. King Edwin was converted and baptised on 11th April 627 'the Birthday of the Northumbrian Church'. Domneva's two aunts, Eanswith and Eocengota, both devoted their lives to the Church. Eanswith founded a Convent at Folkestone and Eocengota went to France, to the monastery at Farmoutier-en-Brie. Perhaps the greatest influence on Domneva at the time of her betrothal to Merewald was her cousin Eormenhild who had married King Wulfhere of Mercia. She had gone to live at Tamworth, the royal seat of the Mercian dynasty. Domneva might have been comforted to feel that someone close to her in age and in family ties was living not far from her in the remote West.

And so, the long journey to the Magonsaetan began. It is probable that Domneva had travelling with her, a retinue of slaves and servants and a number of kinsfolk concerned with her safety and happy arrival. 'Within the legal framework that developed in Anglo-Saxon England a woman's rights and her future, as she moves from one family to another are carefully protected. It is not, as in some societies, that she moves from the 'authority' of a father to that of a husband. On the contrary, she retains within her marriage the support of the family she was born into.' (Fell, 1986) We can envisage quite a large crowd journeying together in that royal party.

The chronicles of Anglo-Saxon times offer many examples of the great distances that people travelled in and around England and to countries on the Continent. In England 'One of the chief legacies of Rome was a system of roads, built so that Roman armies and merchandise could move quickly about the country. These well-constructed roads were used by the Anglo-Saxons in their ordinary day-to-day business. There can be little doubt that they deteriorated during the Anglo-Saxon period, but the roads must still have been in fairly good condition. The Anglo-Saxons apparently thought of the roads not, as the Romans had done, as a system of trunk communications, but as a means of communication between market towns. Small tracks were developed from the newly-founded villages linking them directly with the nearest town or with the nearest stretch of made road. Along the roads passed messengers and parties of clerics, royal officials and pilgrims, pack-animals and carts carrying merchandise, and the baggage train of the royal court as it moved from centre to centre . . . Whenever possible, however, merchandise was transported by water. This was quicker, less physically exhausting, and cheaper. (Wilson)

It was likely on this occasion that both modes of transport were employed and that Domneva and her party used the same route as Saint Augustine had taken when he went to meet the British Bishops at the River Severn in Gloucester at the beginning of the seventh century. This route would possibly have taken them up the river Thames by boat as far as Cricklade, and then by Anglo-Roman road through Cirencester to Gloucester. David Hill explains in his 'Atlas of Anglo-Saxon England' that due to certain climatic changes the level of the waterways was fractionally higher for a period. Small streams we know today were then navigable in flat bottomed boats and the higher reaches of the rivers could be used for transport. From Gloucester Domneva might have travelled again by boat up the River Severn as far as Wroxeter, or further south up the River Wye to Hereford, or by Anglo-Roman road in either direction to meet her royal bridegroom. On the roads she would have travelled in a wagon, a substantial wooden vehicle with a leather roof and the carts of baggage and passengers would have been drawn by men as well as draught animals. The river boats were 'miniature editions of sea-going vessels', rowing boats with a simple wooden keel. It was a complicated manoeuvre involving many days of travel with rest stops at the different market towns on route: London, Cookham, Dorchester-on-Thames, Wallingford, Oxford, Cricklade, Cirencester, Gloucester, Tewkesbury, Deerhurst, Worcester and so on. Perhaps there was a sense of urgency to get the journey over, to deliver the illustrious passenger and her valuable luggage, gifts of jewels, gold and silver coins (thrymsas and sceattas), linen, wool and silk cloth and books from the Continent.

A clearer picture of Domneva's personal belongings, her garments and jewellry, has been handed down through archaeological and literary evidence and early illustration. 'Finally the coming of Christianity with the mission from Rome and the trafficking between kingdoms which ensued seem to have led to a total change in women's dress during the seventh century. Gone are the old fashions, with their plethora of brooches and great festoons of beads; gone too are the regional differences. The last clear view we have, before grave-finds fail us, is of a uniform culture, with the great ladies of Kent, Wessex, East Anglia and Mercia all dressed alike in a sewn costume, requiring no metal fasteners, with gold and silver jewellry consisting only of delicate chain-linked headdress-pins and elegant necklets of beads and jewelled pendants.' (Campbell)

In her study of 'Dress in Anglo-Saxon England', Gale Owen-Crocker gives a more detailed analysis of women's costume and the fashions that reflected the spread of Christianity and England's links with the Frankish Empire and Mediterranean countries. She gives her own translation of Aldhelm's observations of the elaborate dress of some of the nuns of Barking who appeared to be dressing like secular women. The kind of costume consisted of, 'a linen shirt; a scarlet or violet tunic, hooded, and sleeves striped in purple with silks; the garments are encircled with dark red furs . . . dark-grey veils for the head yield to white and coloured wimples which hang down from the grips of fillets as far as the ankles.' Aldhelm's notoriously complicated Latin description was primarily aimed at stamping out the sinful extravagance of these supposedly Holy women. He even gives us details of their hair style. 'the hair of their forelocks and the curls at their temples are crimped with a curling iron'. (Translation by Michael Lapidge) From his description and from Anglo-Saxon illuminations of that date we get a picture of the style of gown worn by Domneva. They depict a brightly coloured, ankle length robe made of wool and trimmed with bands of embroidery in silk or gold thread. The elbow length sleeves are wide and reveal the tighter sleeves of an under garment. Round her waist she may have worn an eye catching belt and jewelled buckle that seem to have been popular in Kent. The neckline was not low but it may have revealed a necklet or a necklace bearing a cross. Over this gown she may have worn a flowing cloak fastened by a single disc brooch made of gold and garnets. The cloak was hooded but she might also have worn some kind of headdress fastened by pins or brooches. As the young bride was a Princess she may well have worn over her outer garment a 'pendant Bullae' described by Gale Owen-Crocker as 'The most striking feature of seventh century necklaces and one which was certainly a Frankish fashion and copied from Byzantine models . . . They were almost certainly a symbol of rank . . . a jewelled collar, fringed with drop-shaped pendants as well as a string of jewels above it.' Domneva's other jewellery may have included finger and arm rings; she may have carried trinkets at her belt, tweezers, keys and a comb and a cylindrical metal box containing relics.

Later in her life we may have found Domneva dressed in the sombre colours that became increasingly appropriated by Church devotees and her jewellery used to embellish ecclesiastical vestments. But on the occasion of her marriage such a sumptuous display of adornment would have added to her status and given the power of wealth to her royal bearing.

The royal quarters of the young King and Queen of the Magonsaetan were unlikely to have been built on such a grand scale as those built for the Northumbrian Kings at Yeavering. There the huge king's hall was surrounded by smaller but still impressive rectangular buildings and a large Roman styled amphitheatre which could have seated as many as three hundred and twenty people on a royal occasion. Archaeological surveys of a number of Anglo-

35

Saxon sites in other parts of the country, Cheddar, Cowdery's Down and so on, give evidence of substantial buildings constructed with such style and sophistication they must have been the 'halls' belonging to people of wealth and importance. No royal site has been unearthed in the region ruled over by Merewald but there is every likelihood that his own royal residence was also a rectangular building of wood and wattle walls. A double line of posts would have supported a roof of thatch or wooden tiles through which the smoke escaped from a central fireplace. The largest building or king's 'hall' might have had a screened off room at one end. It would have been grouped around by similar buildings of a smaller size. The household goods recorded in the wills and bequests of wealthy people of the time include wall coverings, bedsteads and bed clothes, table linen and many chests containing soft furnishings. Domneva's accommodation was certainly not as sophisticated as the royal house of Kent where new and more advanced architectural methods were being introduced from the Continent. However we learn from Goscelin's account that she entered into her husband's building programme following his conversion, of 'Constructing for God churches all over'. It is said that 'both King and Queen, his companion, constructed the monastery at Gloucester to the glorious martyr and King Saint Oswald which by them both was not only increased by generous possessions but also adorned with such ornaments that because of the abundance of its decorations it was commonly called "Golden".'

VI

'664. In this year there was an eclipse of the sun on 3rd May; and in this year a great pestilence came to the island of Britain, and in that pestilence Bishop Tuda died, and was buried at Wagele. And Eorcenberht, king of the people of Kent, died, and his son Egbert succeeded to the kingdom. And Colman went with his companions to his own land. And Ceadda and Wilfrid were consecrated, and in the same year Archbishop Deusdedit died.' *Anglo-Saxon Chronicle*

'He that dwelleth in the secret place of the most High shall abide under the shadow of the almighty.

I will say of the Lord, he is my refuge and my fortress: my God; in him will I trust.

Surely he shall deliver thee from the snare of the fowler, and from the noisome pestilence.

He shall cover thee with his feathers, and under his wings shalt thou trust: his truth shall be they shield and buckler.

Thou shalt not be afraid for the terror by night; nor for the arrow that flieth by day;

Nor for the pestilence that walketh in darkness; nor for the destruction that wasteth at noonday.' *Psalm 91*

'And first an hour of mournful musing,
And then a gush of bitter tears,
And then a dreary calm diffusing
Its deadly mist o'er joys and cares;
And then a throb, and then a lightening,
And then a star in heaven brightening –
The star, the glorious star of love.' *Emily Brontë*

664 was a dark year for Britain. The 'disappearance' of the sun in May must have seemed to many a dreadful omen foretelling the bitter outcome of the invasion of the bubonic plague that secured so many victims. It was a year of darkness and death. Although Christianity was by then the dominant religion the plague seemed to be no chooser between saint and sinner. In its clutches many despaired and reverted to heathenism, there seemed to be no end to the suffering. So soon after the great Synod of Whitby, that coming together of the factions within the Church, two of its revered bishops caught the plague and died, Deusdedit, the sixth Archbishop of Canterbury and Tuda, Bishop of Lindisfarne. King Eorcenberght of Kent too fell victim and died of the dreaded disease, he who had ruled for twenty four years and had rid his kingdom of all pagan idols. The Church was badly stricken, many of its leaders were carried off by the pestilence that depopulated whole monasteries. A new generation was called upon to keep the Light of Christianity bright, Egbert inherited the crown of Kent and continued in his father's footsteps, Bishop Ceadda was consecrated Bishop of York and Wilfrid Bishop of Ripon. In the far West a new 'star' was brightening the skies when Domneva gave birth to her daughter Milburga.

Milburga was the first-born, she had a younger sister Mildryth about whom much has been written. Domneva and Merewald had four children, Milburga, Mildryth, Mildgith and Merefin. Their names alliterate with one another and with the name of the Kingdom as was the custom chosen by dynasties in the Anglo-Saxon period. Merefin, their last child, was their only son and was 'carried from here in his infancy, and God transferred him to the joys of the innocents'. (Goscelin. Vita Milburga, trans. Workman)

Meanwhile the work of spreading Christianity through-out the Magonsaetan was Merewald's and Domneva's su-preme task. Goscelin describes their relationship to each other and to this work as, 'the delight of the flesh was put second and heavenly conversation put first.' It is also recorded that Merewald granted lands and property to be used for religious communities. He 'constructed for God churches all over, and when they were built he gave them rich farms and "families". (Goscelin) It is not known whether these pockets of land were guaranteed to the owners by charter, 'book right', to be passed down within the family. In a society that was not yet organised around a local parish church and priesthood these 'family monasteries' played an invaluable role in bringing the layman directly into touch with the Christian way of life and the monastic ideal. How strict were the rules prescribed within these 'families' has not been recorded. 'This was an age in which a close connection existed between family pride and religious devotion. Some of the pagan shrines of the Anglo-Saxons seem to have been family affairs and some of their monasteries were likewise so.' (Mayr-Harting)

Merewald's interest in the monastic life was no doubt influenced by his association with Saint Botulf, the highly respected Abbot from East Anglia whose reputation spread as far as the Magonsaetan. The Anglo Saxon Chronicle records that in 654 'Botulf began to build the minster at Icanho'. This monastery became a famous example for other religious houses to follow but it is not known how Botulf's influence in Merewald's kingdom began. According to Dr. Finberg, 'Great as was its renown in Botulf's day, we should never have suspected a relationship between this East Anglian house and Milburga's abbey far away in the west midlands. But it is hard to imagine any period in the history of Wenlock when a fiction of such relationship would have been invented'. The early land charter records how the monastery at Icanho played such an important role in the founding of the religious house at Much Wenlock. It states 'in 675–690 Edelheg, Abbot of Icanho, with the consent of Saint Botulf's convent to the nun Milburga. 144 'manentes' in various places, including 97 in the place called Wimnicas (Much Wenlock)'. This generous endowment is recorded more fully in Milburga's own Testament. 'in the name of my Lord Jesus Christ, I Edelheg, Abbot of the monastery called Icanho, with the consent of the whole household of Abbot Botulf of holy memory, give to the consecrated virgin Milburga an estate of ninety seven hides in the place called Wimnicas, and in another place, by the River Monnow, an estate of twelve hides, and in another place called Lydas and estate of thirty hides, to be for ever at her own disposal, so that in accordance with the monastic rule of life she may have full power, living or dying, to bestow the land on any one she may choose, but on condition that the aforesaid place shall be by the grace of God remain unalterably under the tutelage of the church of the worshipful Abbot Botulf, not under compulsion but of its own accord, since it is with the money of that same church that the land is being purchased from the king named Merewald.' The signing of this charter forged a link that promised to be strong, between the religious houses of Icanho and Much Wenlock. Moreover Merewald appears to have accomplished a business transaction over the purchase of the land for the foundation of his daughter's monastery.

Milburga was then still a child, she had yet to be educated for the work that lay ahead but unexpected and traumatic events were about to change the course of her family life. Goscelin described the changes that were occuring in her parents' relationship which finally led to their separation.

'At last therefore King Merewald and his royal companion Domneva after giving birth to the aforementioned children began to grow weary of ordinary embraces. Therefore by grace of celibacy and by mutual agreement they abstained from carnal intercourse. Christ was the heir of all their possessions as they were co-heirs of his eternal blessedness. O how glorious, what an excellent example of holiness! . . . So just as a dove when freed from the nets flies to a friendly town, so the noble queen Domneva free from the bonds of the flesh, returned to her native Kent. And there like the evening star returning from its setting, she became again the morning star arising, never again to be the evening star. More delighted therefore by the sepulchral halls of her first tutor Augustine and his companions than by the royal palaces of the region of Mercia of which she had been chief and queen.'

And so the royal separation was agreed upon by mutual consent and nothing further was recorded of its possible affect upon the immediate family or upon the kingdom of the Magonsaetan. But a far more violent event prompted Domneva's accelerated return to Kent. Her princely brothers, Aethelred and Aethelbert were brutally murdered at the Kentish royal house and Domneva went immediately to claim her 'wergild', a payment due by law to the nearest relation or family of any injured or murdered person, man or woman. David Rollason gives an account of the gruesome story and the remarkable events that followed in his study of the 'The Mildrith Legend' taken from Goscelin's original text of 'The Life of Saint Mildrith'.

'Aethelred and Aethelbert were orphans and entrusted to King Egbert, son of their paternal uncle Eorcenberht and his wife Seaxburg. The princes' wisdom and virtue offended Thunor one of the king's counts and his most valued attendant on his children, who feared that they would become dearer to the king than he. He suggested to the king that they might deprive him or his children of the kingdom and sought permission to kill them secretly. The king refused because they were relatives and dear to him. But Thunor asked many times and eventually murdered them secretly and buried them in the king's throne. Going out at cock-crow, Egbert saw a beam of light standing up through the roof of the hall. Terrified, he forced Thunor to tell him the whereabouts of the bodies. He then called his witan (councillor) and, with the support of Archbishop Deusdedit he summoned Domneva to choose a wergild for them. She chose eighty hides on Thanet and crossing over the river with the King she demanded as much land as her hind would run around. The king consented and he and Domneva followed the hind until they came to Thunor's 'hleaw', where Thunor tried to dissuade the king from making the grant but the earth opened and swallowed up the jealous Count.

In Domneva's case the king paid on behalf of the victims' murderer Thunor the sum of eighty hides of land, a substantial payment, appropriate for two members of the highest class of early Anglo-Saxon society. It may have been a prudent move on Domneva's part to use her pet hind to mark out the boundary; she must have known, far more than the king, her animal's running abilities! In any case she secured a large area of land on which she built a monastery, dedicated to Saint Mary, and 'gathered virgins there'. It is impossible to speculate whether Domneva would have left the Magonsaetan if the murder of her brothers had not precipitated her return to Kent. However the separation from her husband was accomplished in a way that assured Domneva all the blessings she needed, from the Church and from her illustrious family, to establish the style of religious life she most desired.

In the meantime Milburga and her two sisters had also left their father's home and had been brought to Kent with their mother. It would be misleading to imagine what affect such traumatic events had on three young children then aged about twelve, ten and eight. The breakdown of their parent's marriage, their removal to an unfamiliar part of the country, the horrible death of their two uncles and their mother's decision to embrace a monastic way of life may have had some direct impresssion on the decisions they made later on in life. More immediate was the decision to send them over to France to be educated at the monastery of Chelles, north of Paris. At the time Domneva and Merewald may have had anxieties about their children's safety. War was disrupting the peace in Mercia. King Wulfhere had been slain in battle in Northumbria in 674 and Ecgfrith, son of King Oswiu of Northumbria had become Mercia's Overlord. Other Kentish royal children in a previous generation had been sent over to France for their safety. Queen Ethelburga sent her infants when she fled, widowed, to the south in 633. More possibly the decision was made to send these young daughters 'in accordance with the prevailing custom for English ladies and girls of noble birth to be educated in Gallic convents.' (Jackson and Fletcher, 1965) Bede is more specific about the reason for this custom when he writes in his 'Ecclesiastical History', 'at that time but few monasteries were being built in the country of the Angles, many were wont, for the sake of monastic conversation, to repair to the monasteries of the Franks or Gauls; and they also sent their daughters there to be instructed and delivered to their heavenly bridegroom.' There can be no doubt that Milburga's education was to have a lasting influence on her life.

The convent of Chelles on the outskirts of Paris was founded by Bathilde, wife of Clovis II of France in 673. This remarkable woman was born in England and taken over to Gaul as a slave-girl. She was renowned for her intelligence and beauty, qualities that brought her to the attention of the King who subsequently made her his wife. She acquired formidable political power and influence at his court. Van Lantschoot records in 'Dictionaire d'Histoire et de Geographie Ecclesiastique' that 'une tache semble avoir obscuri le beau tableau de cette régence éminemment Chrétienne'. It seems that she was not above arranging assassination to further her ends and was even denounced by some as a 'Jezabel'! Be that as it may, Bathilde did much to enlarge and furnish the convent of Chelles where she retired towards the end of her life and where she was venerated for her devotion and asceticism. The revelation of the darker side of her character is only one example of how human frailty crept into religious life. It may help to explain the deplorable experiences Milburga's younger sister, Myldrith, suffered while she was at Chelles. Lina Eckenstein relates this legend in 'Woman Under Monasticism' p. 86, ending with a quotation from 'Lives of Women Saints'

43

(written about 1610) edited by Horstman for the Early English Text Society, London 1887.

'According to her legend, Mildrith, by far the best known of the sisters, was sent abroad to Chelles for her education, where abbess Wilcoma wished her to marry her kinsman, and on the girl's refusal cast her into a burning furnace from which she came forth unharmed. The girl sent her mother a psalter she had written with a lock of her hair (torn out by the infuriated Wilcoma). She made her escape and arrived in England, landing at Ebbsfleet. "As she descended from the ship to the land and set her feet on a certain square stone the print of her feet remained on it, most life-like, she not thinking anything; God so accomplishing the glory of his handmaid. And more than that; the dust that was scrapen off thence being drunk did cure sundry diseases." '

The reputation of Chelles seems not to have been tarnished by this incident and it is not mentioned in Goscelin's 'Life of Saint Milburga'. More is known about the monastery's prestige; Saint Botulf of Icanho was an early student there, and the illustrious Hilda of Whitby was planning to take her vows there when Aidan persuaded her to stay in the north of England. Chelles offered an education in languages, music, embroidery, calligraphy, Bible study and church liturgy and its cellular structure inspired the form of other religious houses in England. 'More than one Anglo-Saxon monarch wrote asking that disciples might be sent from Chelles to found convents for men and women in England.' (Levison, 1913) Merewald sent such a request for someone to help him to set up the monastery at Much Wenlock. Possibly Botulf had a hand in persuading him of the convent's excellence. It is recorded that a young woman named Liobsynde, a Frankish name, went over to the Magonsaetan to perform that task.

VII

'The great honour paid by Christianity to the celibate life and the wide field of action opened to a princess in a religious house were strong inducements to the sisters and daughters of kings to take the veil.'   *L. E. Eckenstein*

'Inside the monastery walls, where surrogate and natural mothers, natural daughters and daughters in Christ shared high monastic office, which they often handed down as a precious privilege, we are vividly reminded that women's groups are nothing new. Given the brutal bond that earthly marriage at the time often proved to be, the wish to be a Bride of Christ in genteeler circumstances hardly comes as a surprise.'   *N. Herman*

'Serene will be our days and bright
And happy will our nature be,
When love is an unerring light,
And joy its own security.'   *Wordsworth*

After a decade there emerges a picture of the three daughters of Merewald and Domneva, their convent education and their devotion to the Church complete, they had made their decision to be 'Brides of Christ'.

Mildrith, it is recorded, joined her mother at Thanet and later succeeded her as Abbess; she was consecrated together with seventy virgins by Theodore, Archbishop of Canterbury. Both mother and daughter lived and died within the convent walls. According to Goscelin 'The famous virgin Mildgith the youngest daughter of her blessed mother Domneva, led a life of holy conversation on the borders of Northumbria, where through her by divine power, were performed many miracles and signs to the praise and glorification of God and to the veneration of her most pure chastity; she cherishing her folk with pious beneficence was a benefit to her faithful people.' As for Milburga, she chose to return to her father's kingdom, to the monastery already set up in her honour and over which she would eventually preside. We can get no idea from written evidence whether there was any pressure put on her to make this decision or whether there was any particularly strong bond between father and daughter. That Merewald had chosen to found a monastery for his eldest daughter at Much Wenlock may point to a special relationship between the two. There is certainly no hint of any unwillingness on Milburga's part to leave the scholastic and more progressive environment of the Frankish religious houses or the convents of Kent, East Anglia and the North East, already established in such places as Whitby, Ely, Barking and Coldingham. Milburga was probably eighteen when she returned to the Magonsaetan from Chelles.

In the meantime the continuance of Merewald's work of spreading the Gospel throughout his kingdom was being recognised. In 680 Archbishop Theodore created the diocese of Hereford as part of his great task of reorganising the diocesan system throughout England and preparing the spiritual unity of the nation. Hereford was already an important fortress town traversed by the river Wye and a Roman road; now its status was considerably heightened. 'The first bishop of Hereford is thought to have been that same Putta, bishop of Rochester, who after the Mercian King's devastation of Kent found refuge with Aethelred's own bishop and was given some land and a church, which may well have been at Hereford. This diocese was almost certainly founded about this time to embrace the tribes of settlers known as the Magonsaetan, across the Severn, inhabiting what must have been a very indeterminate area, with much admixture of the Celtic and Germanic racial stocks.' (Godfrey) Other evidence endorses Putta as Hereford's first Bishop, Florence of Worcester puts him at the top of his list, a fact accepted by W. Bright in 'Early English Church History'. Putta is described by Bede as 'a person better skilled in ecclesiastical discipline, and more addicted to simplicity of life than active in wordly affairs. He was extraordinarily skilful in the Roman style of church music which he had learned from the disciples of the holy Pope Gregory.' (The Ecclesiastical History, Book IV chapter 2.) It was under Putta therefore that the church in the Magonsaetan adopted Gregorian Chant which was beginning to be used by all the English churches although it was an art the Anglo-Saxons found hard to master. But Putta was known to be always 'most ready to go and help those who wished to learn church music.' Years before Putta's consecration at Hereford Merewald had founded a church and a 'double house' at Leominster and this was probably the ecclesiastical centre of the kingdom before Hereford was granted a bishop's see.

The 'double house' or double monastery, was not a mixed community but two adjacent monasteries existing side by side under a single leadership. This idea for religious communal living had spread from the Orthodox east and had certainly taken hold in England before Archbishop Theodore arrived in 668; he voiced his disapproval of such establishments. When Bede wrote about the ravages of the plague at the monastery of Barking he described the men and women as having separate churches, but he also told of the genuine affection existing between them. When the nuns left their oratory they went out to sing over the graves of their stricken brethren. The segragation of the sexes was more strictly held in some places than in others. In Coldingham a scandal grew up around the intimacy between the monks and nuns, especially as the women there were dressing to attract the brethen. When a fire broke out that destroyed the whole house it was thought to have been divine intervention. The nuns under Tetta of Wimborne on the other hand, were not even allowed to be visited by Bishops!

Double monasteries were commonly ruled by abbesses, women of considerable power and influence. Until the ninth century they were possibly the only institutions to make provision for nuns. The system worked well. The abbess and her women ran the domestic arrangements, the men administered the sacraments and did the heavy work; every community was self supporting. In the troubled times of the seventh and eighth centuries when the double monastery was at the height of its popularity, it was a security measure to have a group of strong armed men close to a community of nuns, to ward off any would-be invader. For two generations there was peaceful coexistence between the Magonsaetan and Welsh tribes along its border but that peace had to be carefully monitored. The monastery at Much Wenlock was strategically placed close to the defence position of the Wenlock Edge that over-looked the Welsh neighbourhood.

Botulf and Merewald chose the site for Saint Milburga's monastery carefully and well. It lies in a valley bounded on the west by Wenlock Edge which is the source of the stream which now emerges from the north of the monastery and meanders eastwards along the valley to join the river Severn at Buildwas. To the west are three wells, Saint Owen's well and two others on the monastery side of Bar-row street. Saint Owen's well may have been named after a monk who travelled south with Saint Chad when he was appointed to the Mercian diocese in 684. Barrow street is an early road connecting Wenlock to Barrow, a hamlet a few miles to the south east. There are a fish pond and a pool dam to the west of the monastery.

'Wimnicas' is the old Welsh name for Wenlock, meaning 'white monastery'; it is quite probable that at an early date the walls of the church there were white-washed. In an article written by Humphrey Woods (1987) on recent excavations at Much Wenlock, he tenders the theory that the site was chosen to incorporate a complex of Roman buildings, possibly a large courtyarded villa. There are no signs that such an early settlement had been used after the departure of the Romans and that is why the walls of the villa would have survived. We know from the Anglo-Saxon elegy 'The Ruin' that Roman buildings were still very much in evidence at the time.

'Wondrous is this wall-stone; broken by fate, the castles have decayed; the work of giants is crumbling. Roofs are falled, ruinous are the towers, despoiled are the towers with their gates; frost is on their cement, broken are the roofs, cut away, fallen, undermined by age. The grasp of the earth, stout grip of the ground, holds its mighty builders, who have perished and gone; till now a hundred generations of men have died. Often this wall grey with lichen and stained with red, unmoved under storms, has survived kingdom after kingdom; its lofty gate has fallen . . . the bold in spirit bound the foundation of the wall wondrously together with wires. Bright were the castle-dwellings, many the bath houses, lofty the host of pinnacles, great the tumult of men, many a mead hall full of the joys of men, till Fate the mighty overturned that. The wide walls fell; days of pestilence came; death swept away all the bravery of men; their fortresses became waste places; the city fell to ruin. The multitudes who might have built it anew lay dead on the earth. Wherefore these courts are in decay and these lofty gates; the woodwork of the roof is stripped of tiles; the place has sunk into ruin.'   *translated by A. F. Scott*

If such an abandoned Roman site was at hand the buildings would have been restored by the monks and a room with a niche at the east end converted into a church. These walls would have probably been replastered and white-washed. Builders in this part of the country in the seventh century had not yet the skills of stone building. Those skills were gradually spreading over to England from France and the Mediterranean countries with the ecclesiastical builders of the Roman church. These ready-made buildings, if such existed, would have given the unskilled builders of the Magonsaetan a 'head start'. They were conveniently placed in a sheltered valley with a plentiful supply of fresh water. The nuns and monks' living quarters of wooden huts would have grouped around the church in cellular fashion already in use in Botulf's own monastery at Icanho. Such a theory is open to specualtion and doubt but it lends colour to the all too dim outline of the picture of Saint Milburga's early religious settlement.

It was the nun from Chelles, Liobsynde, whose honour and duty it was to move into the new monastery at Much Wenlock and to lay the foundations of the religious community life there. When Milburga returned to the Magonsaetan (682) it is thought she served under Liobsynde for several years as a Novice before she was elevated to the position of Abbess in 687. But her father had not long to live. Merewald died in 685 and was buried in the crypt at Repton, the burial place of the kings of Mercia. Goscelin writes of the death of the King.

'But Merewald King of the Mercians after the contest of his genuine struggle and the blessed culmination of his life, received the joy of the heavenly life, leaving his body, as is said, at the monastery of Repton, once a fairly well-known place for the conversations of famous men and holy women. This place, in accordance with the meaning of the King's name does not seem to be silent about the excellence of the King. For his name means 'Fold of the Mountain', from which, as it were, he speaks to us. What the memorable King achieved in an earthly vale, overleaping that vale he settled on the heavenly mountain.'

9   *Repton crypt*

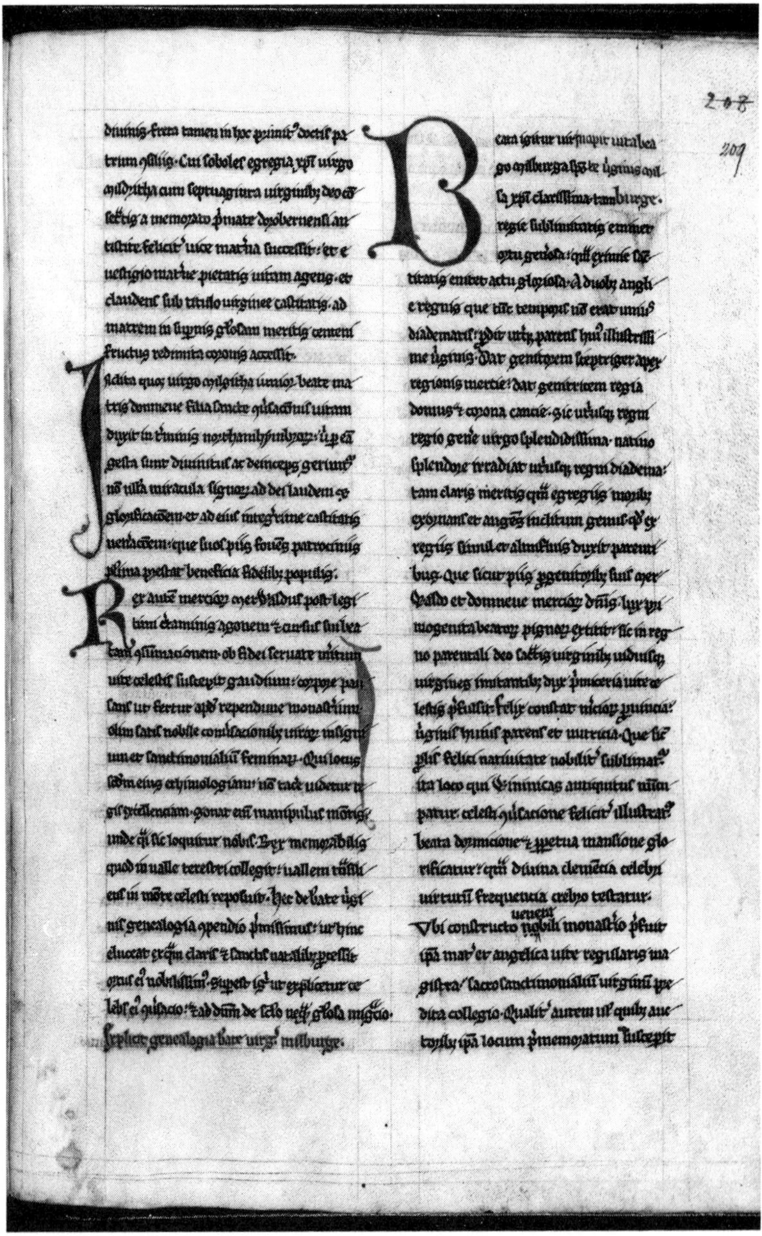

10 *Goscelin: Vita Milburga, Mss. folio 209*

VIII

'Let us all with triumph celebrate this day, and sing to Christ the God alternate hymns. . . Let antiphons with sweet accents strike the ear, and the ode of psalms clang with the double trumpet. . . Let us, brothers, praise the Almighty with accordant voice, and the band of sisters join us in frequent song. Let us give forth under the vault of the temple hymns and psalms and festal responsaries, making melody with the modulations of the psaltery, and strike as the psalmist bids the ten-stringed lyre. Let each one adorn the new shrine with voice, and the brother or sister who reads, the lector, or the lectrix, untie the sacred volumes.'

From a poem of Saint Aldhelm, translated by G. F. Browne

The antiphony of the monks and nuns rings out through Aldhelm's poems; sounds of worship and praise that might have filled the valley of Much Wenlock when Milburga was finally installed there as Abbess. Liobsynde's work of laying a solid foundation for the religious community was finished and she was 'pensionned off' with an estate of land at Hampton. In 687 Milburga became the monastery's 'leader and angelic mistress of regular life, endowed with a sacred college of devout virgins.' Goscelin wrote this in an age when the double monastery had fallen into disrepute and the worship of the Virgin was at its zenith; he omits any mention of the monks.

The power of the monastery grew and flourished until it could be said that 'Milburga was for the kingdom of West Mercia and for Wimnicas what Hilda was for Northumbria and Whitby, a force to be reckoned with by church and state, a formative influence in the early days of Anglo-Saxon Christianity.' (Edwards) There can be no doubt that Milburga was respected for her royal position but 'For Christ's sake she was endeared with the discipline of a convent, she who had been the famous child of a royal household. She had been mistress of a palace, she was now a slave of a convent. Her raiment was poor in place of royal purple. In place of the royal crown of the kingdom she wore the humble veil of the convent. Worthy of proclamation and praise was the change of the royal virgin. How famous was her victory with which she subdued all traces of her royal descent while she put the convent before the palace, a nun's habit before purple, a veil before a crown. Setting everything of the world at nought the celibate virgin triumphed. She was a great joy to the dwellers in heaven with her celibacy and in her person taught celibacy to those on earth. To both heaven and earth dwellers she was a sweet sight'. (Goscelin). Milburga was famous for her beauty, elegance and intelligence, qualities she chose not to trade for a marital position, as we shall see, but which she used to enhance her qualities of leadership.

Some light on Milburga's lively religious house can be gained by looking at the monastic way of life designed by Saint Benedict in Italy in the sixth century. 'On the whole, we are probably justified in believing that by c. 700 at most houses the benedictine Rule influenced the character of the Life.' (Godfrey) The religious practices and regulations for living conditions and work activities set down by Saint Benedict may have been applied in part by Milburga for her double monastery. His idea was that a monastery was 'a school for the service of God', in which a postulant was required to promise not only celibacy and poverty, but also obedience to the abbot or abbess and life-long membership. There would have been no privacy within the two separated parts for men and for women, and the property of the monastery was corporately held. Monks shared in the agricultural and domestic work of the community as did the women, and as far as was possible it was self sufficient with its own water, mill, gardens and bakery. The life was simple and hard, holding very much the same standards as that of the contemporary peasant. The monastic dwelling houses were not specially designed, they would have resembled the ordinary type of wood and wattle huts used by the country folk of the district. The monks and nuns 'houses' were placed on different alignments at Much Wenlock. The open court became the prototype of the medieval cloister. The most important activity of the day was the recitation of the Bible. Just after midnight the night office of nocturns was sung, following the example of the psalmist, "At midnight I will rise to give thanks unto thee." Work in the fields took up most of the day, with spoken prayers at three hourly intervals. Vespers was sung at the end of the day's work, and the day itself closed with reading from sacred books and night prayers. On Church fast days there was only one meal after vespers. On less important fast days the single meal was earlier and on feast days and summer 'ferias' the meal was at noon and supper at about six pm. Strict silence was observed in the evening and everyone retired early to bed. Mass was not said daily, only on Sundays and holy-days. Plain clothes were worn, their actual character being decided by the abbot or abbess, according to the climate. Normally a cowl and tunic sufficed, with boots and stockings for the feet. Traditionally the nuns at Chelles wore a white habit but Goscelin describes Milburga in 'a black sanctimonial cloak'. Monks and nuns were permitted to have a mattress to sleep on with two woollen blankets and a pillow. Their beds were regularly searched for private property which was strictly forbidden; the only personal articles they could keep were a knife, pen, and tablets, a needle and a handkerchief. It was a life in which neither the extremes of luxury or hardship could be tolerated.

There can be little doubt that Milburga would have brought back new ideas for her monastery from her years of training at Chelles. She might also have brought with her books, embroideries, relics and church furnishings. We know from literary evidence and from the Bayeux tapestry that wall hangings were widely used in the tenth century, some form of which may well have furnished halls and rooms at an earlier date. These may have been richly ornamented and brought from the orient or more simple local weavings. The Welsh wool trade was flourishing by the eighth century and thick woven capes being exported from England to the continent. Thick wall hangings would have been used for decoration and to hamper the draughts that swept through those chilly halls. It is possible that Milburga brought a glazier over from France with his new skills to make windows for the church as Benedict Biscop had done for his twin monasteries of Wearmouth and Jarrow. Without doubt the ornaments and furnishings of Much Wenlock monastery, the principal religious house of the Magonsaetan, would have outshone the churches previously founded by her mother and father, already known to be richly endowed. Sadly no trace of an ancient library was left after the Viking raiders plundered and demolished a hundred years later. But it is likely that the monastery treasured volumes of the bible and other holy books.

By the seventh century the love of books was growing throughout England. We read of the great collections of Archbishop Theodore and Bishop Wilfred and of the great libraries of Jarrow and Wearmouth. Nearer to the west Aldhelm was writing poetry, books and letters from his monastery at Malmesbury where he was abbot. An amusing story is told of him haggling over the price of a book some French sailors were selling on the beach at Dover. We also read of 'two anonymous pilgrims to Rome who brought back with them "volumina numerosa", before the year 704.' (Levison) The copying of texts of imported books was often the work of nuns who spent many hours of their lifetime bent over their calligraphy. The Scriptorium where they worked was an essential part of the monastic complex. These early copies made at the end of the seventh and the beginning of the eighth centuries were the foundation of what became the famous English book production of the later Anglo-Saxon period.

One letter has survived giving evidence of a possible link between Milburga and two of the greatest Christian writers of Latin prose in her lifetime, Boniface and Aldhelm. Described by Sir Frank Stenton as 'a man of individual genius', Boniface, whose English name was Wynfrith, dedicated his life to missionary work among the heathen of Germany and to reforming the Frankish church. His work centered on the Continent but he kept close links with the Anglo-Saxon churches in England relying on them to send over monks and nuns to assist him in his work and to send him copies of sacred books from the scriptoria of English monasteries. The letters of Boniface that kept him in touch with his teams of missionary workers have been handed down to us, invaluable documents translated in recent times by Emerton and Talbot. This particular letter Boniface wrote to Eadburga who had succeeded Milburga's sister as Abbess of

Thanet when Mildryth died in 700. After an opening greeting Boniface goes on to say,

'You have asked me, my dear sister, to describe to you in writing the marvellous visions of the man who recently died and came to life again in the convent of the Abbess Milburga, as they were revealed to him and were related to me by the venerable Abbess Hildelida. And now, thanks be to Almighty God I am able to fulfill your wish more fully and more accurately because I myself spoke recently with the aforesaid resurrected brother when he returned to this country from beyond the seas. He then related to me in his own words the astounding visions which he saw in the spirit while he was out of the body.'

From this first paragraph it is possible for us to deduce that Boniface may have visited Milburga's monastery himself in order to interview the monk. Prior to this possible visit he tells Eadburga that he heard of the monk's vision from Hildelida, Abbess of Barking, in which case Milburga's direct contact with Hildelida is also feasible. They were both 'Mothers' of religious houses and may have shared their similar experiences from time to time. The full report of this remarkable mystical experience, written by Boniface six centuries before Chaucer wrote his 'Canterbury Tales' and nine hundred years before Bunyan wrote 'A Pilgrim's Progress', is included as an epilogue. It is a reminder of the eloquence of style of some writers, however few, during those 'dark ages', and it stands as a tribute to the spiritual stature of Milburga's monastery, the home of the visionary monk.

Milburga's communication with Hildelida of Barking would have brought her into touch with the writings of Aldhelm, although we cannot rule out the other possibility of her having met him on his diocesan travels in the south west of England, a few days' journey from the south east border of the Magonsaetan. Aldhelm was certainly the most erudite man of his time. He was born in 639 and received a monastic education under the Irish Abbot Maildubh at Malmesbury. Here he learned a unique style of writing that was in vogue among the Irish of the time. Mayr-Harting describes it as a combination of crossword puzzle and certain types of modern poetry! This bizarre style was considered both clever and complex then, as it is now. Aldhelm was a student of Greek and Latin, Roman Law, astronomy and astrology, mathematics and music. He visited Theodore's famous school at Canterbury and the Pope in Rome. He founded monasteries at Frome and Bradford-on-Avon and in 705 was consecrated bishop of Sherborne in Dorset. He died in 709 and was buried in Malmesbury. This great scholar was famous for his correspondence with other scholars of his time, royalty and church leaders. His letters were highly influential. In 686 he wrote in Latin prose to Hildelida and her community of nuns at Barking calling his letter 'De Laudibus Virginitatis'. In it he exhorted them to despise marriage which although it was considered as honourable in Old Testament times was, under the 'new dispensation', to be regarded as less than glorious as 'silver is less than gold and wool inferior to silk'. The chief purpose of his treatise was to castigate the pride of 'high-born' nuns, their dress, their jewellery, their hair styles and above all their attitudes. Such rigorous admonitions may well have served for more than the nuns of Barking and one can imagine Milburga being glad to use such discipline from so high an authority. Perhaps copies of this famous letter were circulated among nuns and Abbesses in different monasteries.

Knowledge of Milburga's links with other monasteries and ecclesiastical centres is subject to supposition. It is likely she would have had close contact with the Bishop of Hereford and would have visited him there on her journeys around the Magonsaetan. Whether news reached her from further afield from the network of monasteries overuled by Wilfred, or whether she was sent reports of the doctrinal movements within the church it is impossible to know. In the year 690 the churches of England mourned the death of

Archbishop Theodore of whom Bede wrote 'his name shall live from generation to generation. For to say all in few words, the English churches received more advantage during the time of his pontificate, then ever they had done before.' Theodore lived to the great age of eighty eight and was succeeded by Bishop Berthwald. How closely Milburga kept in touch with the monastery of Icanho is also impossible to tell. It is apparent in the charter of land given by the monastery of Icanho to Milburga that Abbot Edelheg meant to keep a 'fatherly eye' on the running of the daughter monastery at Wimnicas. Whether contact was maintained between this richly endowed monastery and the Papacy in Rome is not possible to say. The only record of a pilgrimage from Milburga's religious house is that of the visionary monk who Boniface described as having travelled 'beyond the seas'. He may have joined the inexhaustable stream of pilgrims who crossed Europe into Italy to give thanks for his recovery at the heart of the Roman church.

Goscelin's eulogy of Saint Milburga may seem over embellished and exaggerated to the modern sceptic but it does not prevent our appreciation of the woman who was an outstanding spiritual leader in her day and whose reputation reached far ahead into the middle ages. He wrote of her position as Abbess being

"worthy of the authority of a 'Mother', found with the dignity of holiness. When she had suitably built a monastery she is put in charge by universal vote and by the votes and assertions of kings and controlled by the duties and blessings of the clergy. The first of these 'controllers' was Saint Theodore, Archbishop of Canterbury. Her father and uncle, Merewald and Wulfhere, famed kings of the Mercians enriched the house of god into whose care she had been ordained abbess, with large possessions of estates and adorned it with various rich endowments and decorated it with many priceless relics of Saints so that it resembled the celestial house where nothing might seem to be lacking to those who fear God and faithfully serve

Him. It was forcibly subjected to no earthly power and no servitude within was owed by her to anyone except of their own will. The holiness of the virgin maximised all these decorations and adorned it even more by her own holiness. Just as therefore she had worthily undertaken the position of 'Mother' in herself so also she energetically performed the duties of Mother. So from day to day the sacred ministry of the virginal family grew and the love for the excellent virgin grew more fervent. The pious Mother elect rejoiced, co-elected from the common daughters, dedicated to God by conversion, betrothed to God by declaration. Her flock rejoiced in their turn and in turn the love for the pious Mother and the affection within the family was congratulated. Whence it happened that the house became like an Elysian home or rather like Paradise while in it, as free as it was prosperous, the pursuit of holiness and virtue so flourished that the sanctity of those who lived there together would have graced the high kingdom of heaven. The celibate conversation of those who lived there was happy and joyful. But so that the holy habit might never seem cheap to them or that their virginal minds might never stray from Christ's chastity the holy Mother showed them a light of humility to be imitated. Indeed she was more truly their Mother and mistress because she was the humble provider and servant of them... The excellent Milburga peceived wisdom which, when she saw it, she put in front of kingdoms and positions and she thought riches as nothing compared with it. She chose it as if it were the mother of all good things and loved it beyond safety and beauty. For taught by her divine reading and by the unction of the Holy Spirit, she knew that no one who was without it would be participant in the divine mercy. The learned Milburga embraced wisdom and sought after it from her youth... The wisest Virgin knew the sciptures because wisdom is not found on earth among men who live softly. She girded up her loins like a brave warrior and allowed herself no indulgence in earthly pleasure. She sought nothing too pleasurable in eating, nothing over luxurious in clothes and she only kept out hunger and cold with a bit of each cast-off... so she perpetuated in herself the splendour of her shining works and the sun of eternity."

Like many of her female contemporaries, abbesses from the ruling class, Milburga was provided with a 'dominion' to rule at Much Wenlock double monastery. In her religious family she could find comparitive safety in numbers and fellowship among men and women inspired by Christian zeal, although monasteries were by no means always 'safe havens'. Under her men and women proceeded to work together in the cloister as likewise they had done in secular life. But the religious house often provided a refuge from an unwanted or unattractive partner in an age of arranged marriages and enabled women to avoid child bearing. All over England double monasteries came to be used as 'old people's homes' for the aging nobility and hotels for reputable travellers, orphanages and boarding schools. They 'must have been the greatest single blessing bestowed by Christianity on God's seventh-century Englishmen' (Nicholson)

IX

'This outer world is but the pictured scroll
  Of worlds within the soul,
A coloured chart, a blazoned missal-book
  Whereon who rightly look
May spell the splendours with their mortal eyes
  And steer to Paradise.'

Alfred Noyes

'Charters of the 7th and 8th centuries, granting land to, or for the foundation of, 'monasteria', convey to them extensive endowments. These estates were defined by anciently established boundaries within which were to be found all the natural resources necessary to life. They were frequently assessed at a large number of hides, and included a number of separate settlements dependent on the named central one.'

J. Croom

'One of the facts which we have found out we do not re-word with our pen, but we submit in the same words with which it was originally stated and that we read was partly dictated by the blessed and memorable virgin while she was alive and left by her descendants to be a testament to the transaction by which she obtained the site for her monastery and to be a testament of the donations and exchanges by the purchase of which she acquired for her monastery very many possessions under eminent witnesses and royal authority is clear in what follows.'

Goscelin

At the very end of her life Milburga gathered her family together to listen and to be witness to her final will and testament. Her triumphant years as head of one of the richest and most powerful monasteries in the west of England were over. She had enjoyed power and prosperity and now she knew she was approaching the Paradise towards which her whole life had been steered. Her words were carefully taken down by the scholars of Much Wenlock and miraculously preserved over the turbulent centuries that followed until Goscelin faithfully copied and produced them as part of his 'Vita Milburga'. Professor Finberg's reappraisal of this document thirty years ago opened up a totally new chapter of history not only of Milburga herself but of the local distribution of land and the personages responsible for the gifts of property. In his own words,

'In Shropshire the harvest would have been meagre indeed but for the discovery of one extremely interesting document. The so-called Testament of Saint Milburga, published for the first time in Chapter X, incorporates passages which show every sign of having been transcribed verbatim from five authentic ancient charters.'

It seems appropriate to include Milburga's Testament in full, translated as it is by Prof. Finberg, thereby to carry on the tradition of its remaining intact for over twelve centuries.

"Experience has taught us that the laudable plans and worshipful utterances of our forefathers can sometimes become of no avail to future generations, though executed in due form at the time, since memory slips from the tongue if knowledge of these things is not renewed, for those who can read, by documentary evidences put in writing at the earliest possible time and attested by several witnesses. For this reason I, Milburga, lowly handmaid of Christ, mistress of the monastic way of life, am resolved to set forth, at the very beginning of this little record, and to confirm by the respect due to written attestations, all the landed estates which by the grace of God I possess, and how or by what benefactors they were granted to me, lest my death incur discredit through ignorance of the church's property, and my successors be disturbed by the venomous attacks of envious men.

First of all, I acquire this place called Wimnicas, as several witnesses can prove, by the joint consent of the two parties to whom authority over the place belonged. That is to say, I gave to the worshipful abbot Edelheg and to the religious abbess Liobsynde, in exchange for the aforesaid place, an estate of sixty hides at the place called Hampton; and the abbot, for confirmation of this exchange, caused a charter to be written for me, which reads as follows.

"In the name of my Lord Jesus Christ, I Edelheg, abbot of the monastery called Icheanog, with the consent of the whole household of Abbot Botulf of holy memory, give to the consecrated virgin Milburga an estate of ninety-seven hides in the place called Wimnicas, and in another place, by the River Monnow, and estate of twelve hides, and in another place named Magana an estate of five hides, and in the district called Lydas an estate of thirty hides, to be for ever at her own disposal, so that in accordance with the monastic rule of life she may have full power, living or dying, to bestow the land on any one she may choose, but on condition that the aforesaid place shall by the grace of God remain unalterably under the tutelage of the church of the worshipful Abbot Botulf, not under compulsion but of its own accord, since it is with the money of that same church that the land is being purchased from the king named Merewald." This gift was confirmed by the signatures of 'Abbot Edelheg, Archbishop Theodore, King Ethelred, Bishop Seaxwulf, Abbot Ethelric, King Scotmerchelm, and Mildfrith his brother.' To sum up: the land of this minster include one hundred and forty-four hides.

After this charter of donation, set forth above, I declare that I gained possessions of several landed properties in sundry places by sundry gifts of my brothers King Merchelm and Mildfrith, conveyed by word of mouth, but not without the assent and signature of the most excellent King Ethelred, my uncle. The charter of these donations is to the following effect.

"By the grace of God, I, Merchelm, and I, Mildfrith, with the consent of the most excellent King Ethelred, give to you, our own sister Mildburg, part of the land which by the bounty of the good Lord is ours by right: namely, sixty hides in divers places, to be at your own disposal, so that you may hold, give away, or exchange it at your pleasure. Part of this land is situated around Clee Hill, part by the River Corve, part in the place named Kenbecleag, and part in the place called Chelmarsh. I, Merchelm. I, Ethelred. I, Mildfrith have underwritten this".

When these transactions had been lawfully effected, King Ceolred, of high renown for the pre-eminence of his monarchy, gave me an estate of four hides called Penda's Wrye. The following document refers to this donation.

"Our Lord Jesus Christ reigning over us and guiding us, I, King Ceolred, give to you, Abbess Mildburg, under written assurance, an estate of four hides, to be for ever at your own disposal, so that henceforth you may have free power to give it away or exchange it as you may deem advantageous." This was underwritten by "King Ceolred, Bishop Cedda, Abbot Elric, and Ealdorman Edbrect."

Some time later the consecrated woman and servant of God Feleburg gave me an seate of eight hides, and at the same time also offered me, of her own free will, the charter she received in proof of the (original) donation, to the following effect. "King Coenred, for the redemption of 'his soul', gave to the servant of God Feleburg an estate of hides in Lingen (Lye), to be at her own disposal," these witnesses being present and consenting: "Bishop Tyrhtel, Wihictsi, and Eadbert."

I also bought a property from the king's follower Sigward. To him I gave a large sum of money, and he gave me an estate of three hides, with its charter, called Magdalee. This purchase was attested and underwritten by "King Ethelbald, Bishop Wealhstod, Bishop Wilfrith, Abbot Ova, and Ealdorman Cynric."

Through all the land-books the final utterance of the princes who made these donations and of the witnesses who consented to them is as follows. If any one, be he king or bishop or personage of any rank whatsoever, shall attempt to gainsay these donations and make bold to infringe, in whole or part, this gift consecrated to God, let him be accursed at the coming of the Lord. Amen."

These stern words of Milburga served to preserve the sanctity of the endowments to her church. Over the years they were repeated and read out to the monastic community and church congregations with the same solemnity as was given to readings from the holy scriptures. There was no reason to be ignorant about the exact extent and boundaries of these properties and no doubt that their acquisition was above suspicion. Later it was in the hands of the hagiographer, Goscelin, to endorse these materialistic claims of the church and to assist in protecting them against the hands of acquisitive laymen. His praises for the Saint, his accounts of her miraculous deeds and endeavours gave weight to the truthfulness of the charters. Note that the tradition of 'bannering' the boundaries of the Wenlock franchise, land under the jurisadiction of the Prior of Wenlock, continued until the beginning of the nineteenth century. An account of its happening is given by the Rev. Hartshorne in 'Salopia Antiqua', published in 1841. The bailiff and recorder with men and boys on horseback rode round the extensive boundaries and the town clerk read some sort of 'rigmarole' which they called their charter, from the pillory in Wenlock. One part of it went like this,

'We go from Beckbury and Badger to Stoke on the Clee,
To Monkton, Round Acton and so return we.'

Milburga's land properties were substantial. In all she had been given 219 hides or 'manentes' of land covering ten areas of the Magonsaetan, in five separate charters. The exact measurement of the Anglo-Saxon hide is not known but it is assumed to have been the estate of one household, the amount of land sufficient for the support of one family. This sufficiency was dependent on the original quality and condition of the soil, the climate and accessibility of water, so as a measurement the hide may have altered from one part of the country to another. It has been agreed that the hide may have covered anything between sixty to one hundred and twenty acres of land. In either case Milburga's charters state that she owned many thousands of acres, some in rich alluvial valleys, some forested areas and some on the higher hills.

Since Roman times there had been a gradual erosion of the forests that covered the British Isles. Many vast areas still remained in Anglo-Saxon times, the forests of Dean, Wyre, Morfe and Kinver to name a few. Timber was used for building material, fencing and fuel. Piece by piece the forests were being cleared to make way for crop growing and grazing. Steadily the ploughman, referred to in the Exeter book as 'the old enemy of the wood' was turning over the soil, felling the trees and burning the undergrowth in his path although King Ine's (of Wessex) code of 690 imposed heavy fines on unlawful clearing and burning of trees. In Milburga's lifetime the forests were still rich feeding grounds for the Anglo-Saxon pig, a long-legged animal valuable for its meat. These pigs fed on acorns and beech-mast, grass and berries in the spring and summer and fern roots in the winter. They would have been rounded up into wattle fenced enclosures to be fed and protected as well as allowed to roam free. The forests were the home of wolves, boars, deer and wild cats. They were not safe places for men or their cattle but the honey gatherers must have ventured far and wide in search of wild bees. Honey was used in large quantities for making the mead that flowed into goblets at every festival.

The cleared land, the Anglo-Saxon felds or meadows, were mown for hay to provide winter fodder and they were grazed by domestic cattle. The common felds provided villages with common pasture land for their sheep and cattle; goats and cows are on record and sheep provided milk, wool and meat. Sometimes portions of a large feld would be ploughed and sown. Crops of oats, barley, woad and flax were grown. Oats were fed to calves and foals or made into porridge. Barley was ground and used for bread making. It was also converted into malt for the brewing of beer which was consumed in great quantities. Meat was preserved in salt so there were plenty of thirsty palates to quench! Beans were also grown as an imporrant part of the staple diet. The flax harvest was made into linen or wicks for lamps as was the hemp crop. Woad and madder grew in large quantities to be used for the dyeing of cloth. Herbs from forest and field were in constant use as remedies for common ailments; woad and butter for burns, garlic, onion and goose fat for ear-ache, oak rind and a little worm-wood pounded in ale to get rid of lice, the lousy one having to drink the potion rather than apply it. Remedies were the practiced art of the healer who knew many complicated recipes for ointments and herbal drinks.

If indeed it fell to Milburga as abbess to organise and supervise farmers and workers to maintain her extensive properties her task might well have been an onerous one. Whether she had 'ceorls' and bondsmen or servile 'esnes' to provide a workforce over and above the monks at Much Wenlock, or whether she employed reeves to be in charge of her estates, is not on record. Between the years 688 and 694 a series of laws was drawn up by Ine the king of Wessex, concerning agriculture and to make provision for widows, foreigners and for the protection of the poor. These laws were an important step forward in legislation and they acknowledged Christianity as the basis of all moral and social obligations. Concerning agriculture, Ine stipulated that a 'ceorl', or free husbandman, was allowed to keep and employ domestic servants and slaves and that they in return would receive from him food and shelter. The arable land worked on by ceorls was subject to a 'food rent' payable to the king. Ine's law pronounced that the food rent from ten hides of land should be

'10 vats of honey
300 loaves
12 measures of Welsh ale
30 measures of clear ale
2 full grown cows and 10 wethers
10 geese
20 hens
10 cheeses
A full measure of butter
5 salmon
20 pounds of fodder
100 eels'

Besides this levy there was 'church scot' every householder among Milburga's tenants had to pay each November 11th, after the harvest. This one tenth of the income of all Christians was given to the church for the upkeep of the clergy. Offerings of money delivered at the altar during Mass and fees for burials as well as voluntary tithes were collected by the monastic or minster church serving the particular area. It is likely that Much Wenlock priory paid 'Rome scot', a yearly payment to the papacy.

Ine's laws also governed the employment of slaves, English or Welsh. At the time of the invasion of Britain by the first Anglo-Saxons the early Britons fled into the mountains in the far west. There they settled as 'wealas', or foreigners, a name from which Wales is derived. Many of those left behind became slaves to the Anglo-Saxons. The institution of slavery also included the English peasants since earliest times. Ine made strict rules about slaves and their masters working a six day week. The Sabboth was to be observed and kept 'labourless'. If a master made his slave work on a Sunday he had to set him free and if a freeman worked on a Sunday he stood a chance of being reduced to slavery or having to pay a heavy fine. We can be sure that Milburga 'full of mercy and truly just, rendered to each person pity and justice . . . and did nothing in the desire for empty glory and nothing for the vanity of human praise.' (Goscelin, 'Life of St. Milburga', trans. K. Workman.)

The list of donors and witnesses to the charters granting land to Milburga is impressive. It includes five kings and a prince, six bishops, four abbots, two ealdormen, and a nun. Goscelin was hardly exaggerating when he described Milburga as having been linked to all the top ranking English men of her day; 'Whatever King he was of the virgin's family, no one was in charge in England at that time who was not in some way related to her'.

The first two charters granting the largest properties, one of them the land on which the monastery at Much Wenlock was built, were witnessed by King Ethelred, overlord of Mercia. Ethelred became king in 678 when he defeated Egfrith of Northumbria, Egfrith who had defeated and killed Wulfhere in 674. During Ethelred's reign the ecclesiastical life of Mercia flourished. He was the benefactor of many churches throughout the various provinces of his kingdom. After twenty nine years of reign he retired into the monastery of Bardney in Lindsey where he spent the rest of his life in monastic devotion to the church.

Milburga's large estates of land at Beckbury, Chelmarsh, Easthope and Patton, Barton, Shipton and Sutton were granted to her by King Merchelm and his brother prince Mildfrith. King Merchelm succeeded to the principality of the Magonsaetan after the death of Merewald his father in 685. The name Merchelm is derived from the folk-name Mierce or Merce meaning Mercians and Merchamley in Shropshire is possibly named after him. Merchelm and Mildfrith also witnessed the charter of land given by Saint Botulf's monastery for the founding of Milburga's religious house.

King Coenred enters the story in an indirect way. He succeeded Ethelred in 704 as Overlord of Mercia and all its provinces. His reign lasted only for five years after which he quit the throne and journeyed to Rome where Bede

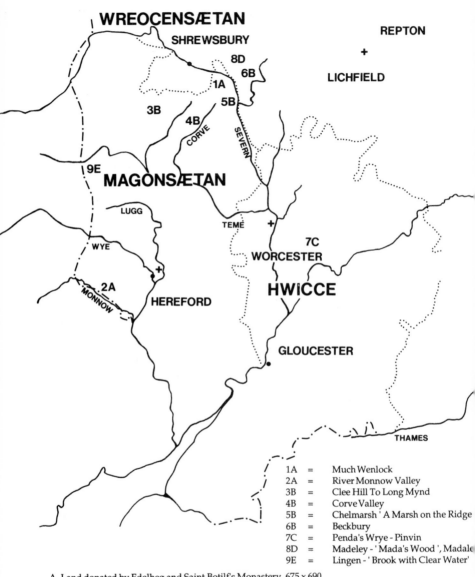

1A	=	Much Wenlock
2A	=	River Monnow Valley
3B	=	Clee Hill To Long Mynd
4B	=	Corve Valley
5B	=	Chelmarsh ' A Marsh on the Ridge
6B	=	Beckbury
7C	=	Penda's Wrye - Pinvin
8D	=	Madeley - ' Mada's Wood ', Madale
9E	=	Lingen - ' Brook with Clear Water'

A. Land donated by Edelheg and Saint Botilf's Monastery. 675 x 690
B. Land donated by Merchelm and Mildfrith. 674 x 704
C. Land donated by King Ceolred. 709 x 716
D. Land donated by Nun Feleburg. 704 x 709
E. Land bought from Sigward. 727 x 736

11   *Location of Milburga's Land Properties*

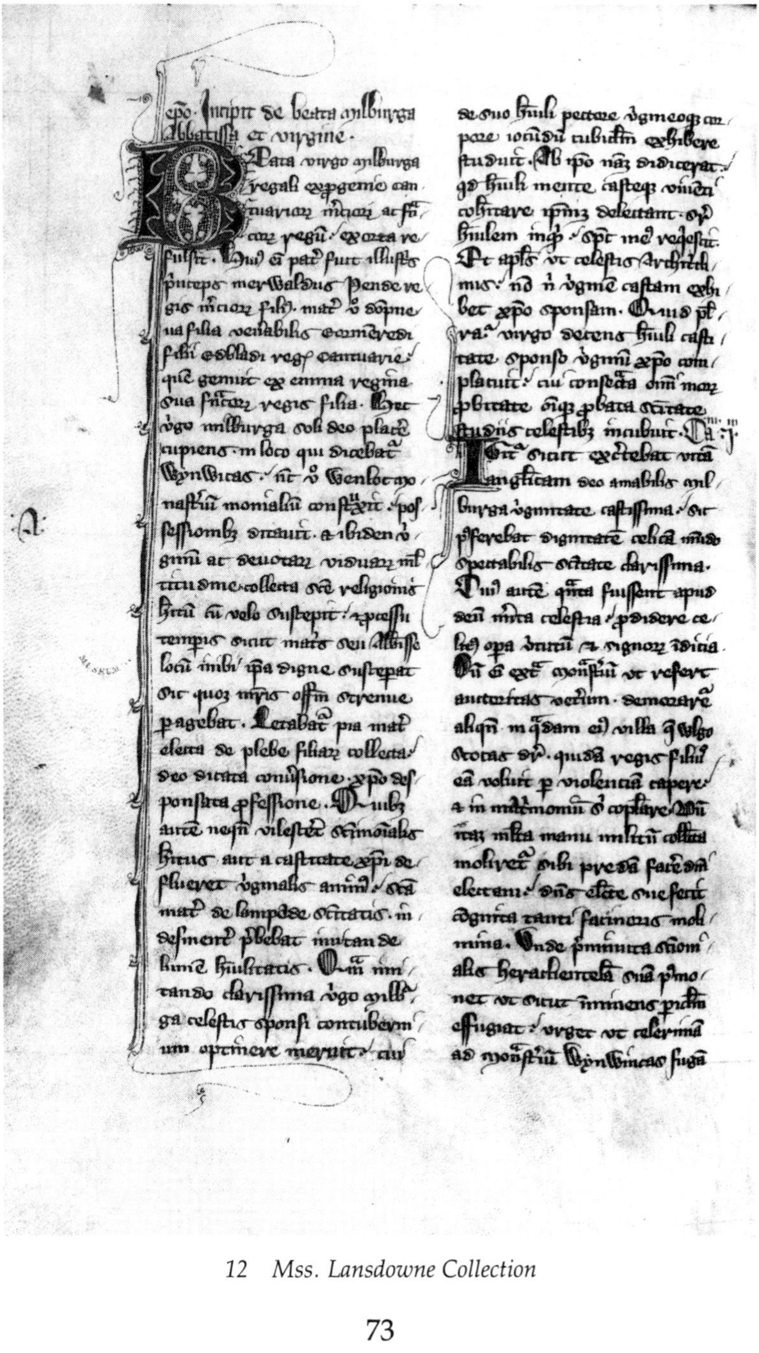

12 Mss. Lansdowne Collection

records, 'he received the tonsure, and became a monk at the shrine of the Apostles, passing the remainder of his days in prayer, fasting and acts of mercy'. (Bede) Before leaving Mercia Coenred offered to the nun Feleburg a gift of land in Herefordshire, at Lye. This he did for the 'redemption of his soul'. Some years later Feleburg gave Milburga both the land and the charter. Professor Finberg observes that there are some remains of a nunnery to be found in that district whose foundation date is uncertain. It is possible that Milburga chose the site for one of her oratories or daughter churches.

Several hundred acres of land at Penda's Wrye, Pinvin or Wyre Piddle, were given to Milburga by King Ceolred a son of Ethelred who succeeded Coenred and reigned from 709 to 716. This king left an evil reputation, and it is noticeable that the Testament refers only to his royal dignity, not to his personal character. 'Already in his lifetime the visionary monk of Wenlock saw demons preparing eternal torment in hell for a king who was believed to be an enemy of monks and too ardent a lover of certain nuns'! (Finberg, trans. S. Bonifatii Epistolae, pp. 14, 152.). The king's evil reputation did not prevent Milburga from accepting his generosity. King Ceolred died insane.

The final king 'related' to Milburga in her land charter was King Ethelbald, grandson of Eowa a brother of the great king Penda. For nearly thirty years Ethelbald held supreme power in southern England as head of a confederation which included Mercia, Wessex and Kent and all the kingdoms between the Humber and the Channel. Early in his life he had been exiled by the wicked king Ceolred and sheltered by Saint Guthlac of Crowland and his companions. Ethelbald came to power in 716 and ruled for forty one years when he was murdered at Seckington near Tamworth. Hie reign was blemished by certain misconduct and he was reprimanded in a letter sent by Boniface and six bishops of English descent living on the Continent. They commended him for his 'good works', alms giving, the repression of robbery, the defence of the poor and the maintenance of peace, "but go on to say; "we have learned from many sources that you have never taken to yourself a lawful wife. So far from being chaste as befits a bachelor, the king has been promiscuous – and these atrocious crimes are committed in convents with holy nuns, with virgins consecrated to God". He is told that even the heathen in Saxony punish women severely for adultery. How much more should an English Christian king be rebuked for these sins! The letter burns with patriotism as well as with moral indignation. Boniface wrote a covering letter to Herefrid, the unfortunate priest who was to read out the rebuke, addressing an illiterate king who was then the most powerful man in England.' (Edwards, 1981) However Ethelbald's reputation was redeemed by the reforms he encouraged within the organisation of the church, in that he freed the church from taxation and assisted in the laying of the foundation of the English parish church system.

Of the six bishops mentioned in the charters, Archbishop Theodore was the most renowned. He witnessed the charter giving land for the foundation of Saint Milburga's monastery as did bishop Seaxwulf, bishop of Lichfield. The Anglo-Saxon Chronicle describes him as 'God's friend and all the country loved him and he was very nobly born and rich in the wordly sense.' Seaxwulf knew a great deal about monastery building. When he was still a monk during Wulfhere's reign, the king commissioned him to finish off constructing the monastery at Medeshamstede, Peterborough, that had been started during Peada's short rule. Seaxwulf lost no time, 'he so sped' that in a few years the monastery was ready and the king was 'very glad'. Seaxwulf became Abbot of Medeshamstede for a period before he was consecrated bishop of Lichfield and during that time this great monastery that had been richly endowed with lands and wealth was given total independence first by the king and then approved by the Pope, meaning that no tax was levied on it. The Chronicle sets down the words of

King Wulfhere, 'This gift is little; but it is my will that they shall hold it so royally and so freely that neither geld nor tribute be taken from it . . . And thus free I will make this minster, that it be subject to Rome alone; and here it is my will that all of us who are unable to go to Rome shall visit St. Peter's (at Peterborough)'. Seaxwulf had been instrumental in one of the early reforms of the organisation of the church. Now as 'bishop to the Mercians' at Lichfield it is likely he played an influential role in the setting up of Milburga's own monastery. The other four bishops who witnessed the conveyances were from the west of England. Bishop Cedda held the see at Lichfield before Seaxwulf was installed there. Bishop Tyrtel was followed by Bishop Wealhstod at Hereford and Bishop Wilfrith, a contemporary of King Ethelbald was Bishop of Worcester.

Of the lay witnesses to the charters, the only personal detail recorded is of Sigward from whom Milburga bought three hides at 'Magdalee', Madeley. He is described as one of King Ethelbald's personal followers and the king himself was witness to the business transaction. The two ealdormen, Edbrect and Cynric have no recorded distinction except for the office they held. Sir Frank Stenton explains in his chapter on 'The Structure of Early English Society', 'Anglo-Saxon England', pp. 301, 302. When the great Mercian kingdom became united under one king in the eighth century, the heirs of many of the lesser dynasties, such as the Magonsaetan, saught favour at the court of the Mercian king. 'Men of this type may often have been allowed to rule their own people under their lord's ultimate authority. But the king who was strong enough could always ignore the claims of a local dynasty, and in course of time men with no hereditary title to rule appeared as ealdormen of provinces that had once been kingdoms. The typical ealdorman of the eighth and ninth centuries was not the heir of a dynasty but a member of the king's household set in charge of a shire, or regio, by his lord and removable at his pleasure . . . Only men of this type, with whom the king was well acquainted, could safely be trusted to lead the fyrd (national militia) of a district, enforce compliance with the judgements of its folkmoots, (local assemblies), and impose terms on local nobles who had allowed their own household men to break the peace.' There can be little doubt that Edbrect and Cynric held important offices and were possibly responsible for the administration of the Magonsaetan towards the end of Milburga's lifetime.

The territorial references in the charters of Saint Milburga's testament lack precision and it is impossible at this distance of time to be precise about the exact whereabouts of all her properties. One place that is mentioned by name is Llanfillo in Wales, five miles north east of Breckon on a small tributary of the Wye, the Lynfi, twelve miles beyond the valley of the Monnow. The church there is dedicated to Saint Milburga. It is quite probable that during the peaceful years of coexistence with the Welsh, Milburga may have established an oratory there, a hundred and sixty miles from Hereford. Milburga might possibly have accomplished that long distance from Much Wenlock to Llanfillo by boat following the River Severn to Chepstow then up the River Wye to Hereford and finally along the Llynfi either by shallow bottomed canoe or by foot along the small river valley. This long route is one example of the great journeys the abbess made around her estates. Another oratory at Stoke Saint Milburga is closely associated with a story that features in one of her legends recounted by Goscelin and the ancient site of another of her daughter churches at Barrow is a comfortable walking distance from Much Wenlock.

Early in the eighth century, during the reign of Coenred, 704–709, the Welsh made devasting raids on the Magonsaetan and the long years of peaceful coexistence came to an end. Welsh envy of the arable plains of Herefordshire and the fertile valleys of Shropshire spilled over from the rugged mountains where it was a struggle to make a living. We are told in the 'Life of Saint Guthlac' that these raids inflicted heavy losses on both sides. Eventually two enormous dykes were built to settle the Mercian – Welsh frontier. Wat's dyke was built early in the eighth century and this was superseded by a larger and longer earthworks planned by king Offa during the second half of his reign between 755 and 796. The date of Wat's dyke is uncertain and we do not know whether the Welsh incursions reached as far as Much Wenlock in Milburga's lifetime. A monastery of such size and importance as hers was undoubtedly an important strategic position and a centre for administration for the surrounding country.

13   *Long Mynd, Carding Mill Valley*

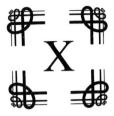

X

'The Chronicler is the history teller . . it will take no effort to gauge the difference between the writer of history, the historian, and the teller of it, the chronicler. The historian is bound to explain in one way or another the happenings with which he deals; under no circumstances can he content himself with displaying them as models of the course of the world. But this is precisely what the chronicler does especially in his classical representatives, the chroniclers of the Middle Ages, the precursors of the historian today. By basing their historical tales on a divine plan of salvation – an inscrutable one – they have from the very start lifted the burden of demonstrable explanation from their own shoulders. Its place is taken by interpretation, which is not concerned with accurate concatenation of definite events, but with the way these are embedded in the great inscrutable course of the world'

Walter Benjamin

'The miracles recorded in a Saint's Life were intended to stimulate the devotion of the reader, to inspire him with a desire to imitate the virtues of which these miracles were the fruit, to provide a little light entertainment perhaps, to illustrate some particular quality and, most important, to demonstrate the Saint's right to the honours of the altar – to his (her) place in the communion of Saints'.

C. W. Jones

The 'Life of Saint Milburga' contains seven miracle stories, four of some length and substance and the last three mere fragments of tales. They were recorded as part of the biography with a view to embellishing the events that actually took place and to encourage an even greater adulation and emulation of the saintly abbess. If indeed Goscelin based these stories on historical support or traditional association we can be permitted to hope that they contain some 'grains of truth' over and above his vivid imagination and remarkable memory. Goscelin was a master of his particular craft as 'chronicler'. He sharpened his quill many times to record the lives of eminent 'holy' men and women up and down the country. Some features in the miracle stories of Saint Milburga appear to be common to those related about other saints of the period when they answer to the popular tradition of saint depicting and legend telling. However we do know that Goscelin did his research thoroughly and that he went to Much Wenlock to collect his material for the biography, so by and large these stories belong uniquely to the Shropshire saint.

The first miracle relates how Milburga defended her virginity and kept her bow intact to belong to God alone. He was her 'heavenly parent' of whose love she could be absolutely sure and with whom she could have a relationship such as had been shown to be entirely sufficient and satisfying not only for her own mother but her two sisters as well. Goscelin's dramatic use of language reinforces Milburga's commitment and reads as well as any escape story.

> 'For while she once was staying outside the Monastery, as the authority of the ancients has it, in one of her towns which is commonly called Stoke, one of the king's sons wished to take her by force and to join with her in wedlock. He was there with a large band of collected soldiers striving to make booty for himself of the chosen of the Lord. The strivings of such a crime were revealed by the Lord to one of His elect (at Stoke) who forewarned warns her visitor (Milburga) to flee with her from

the iminent danger and urges her to make the swiftest flight to the Monastery at Wenlock. Flight is at once prepared, pressed and hurried on. Indeed, the more the virgin feared the danger the quicker she seized escape from the danger, being as wary of the stain of her snow white modesty as shrinking from the joining of the marriage bond. She fled from the man as a dove from the snare, longing for wings with which she might fly to repose and solitude. Solitude is known to no man, solitude is given by God alone. Meanwhile the rash man, defended by soldiers and arms had reached the place where he thought to meet the woman he had desired to seize for himself. But the place was found empty of the presence of the virgin, so the wicked suitor was firstly deceived by her absence and then frightened off by a heavenly miracle. He followed the fleeing lamb of Christ more rabidly than a wolf, but in order that he might not reach the dedicatee to God by any spurious contact he is divinely resisted as he followed.

There was a certain river in the way, called Corf by the natives, crossable by a ford with a fairly shallow bed. The virgin in her flight crossed the river but the man pursuing her could not cross. When the virgin had been put across successfully the river soon grew to such a depth from a sudden storm that it broke its banks and could not be crossed. How did the sacrilegious and wicked pursuer react? Astonished and terrified he suffered well deserved punishment for his rashness. Just as he was denied crossing the river so he was denied contact with the virgin. Confused he turned his back on the fugitive and quicker than he had pursued he fled from her who was was fleeing from him!'

Milburga's best remembered miracle and the one from which she receives her emblem of the goose is this next story of how she rid her lands of these troublesome birds. It might be of special interest to ornithologists and those studying the habits of migratory geese who are known to visit the low lying and coastal regions of Britain during the winter months. These birds may have been the 'Brent' or 'Pink-footed', or more likely the 'Grey Lag' geese, whose very name indicates their longer stay on these islands. Our domestic geese are supposed to have originated from this species that breed on grasslands. They are known to be very wary birds and extremely difficult to approach. Perhaps Milburga's efforts to stop these 'unwelcome visitors' were helped along by the birds' shy and nervous disposition.

'It was winter and the pious virgin the protector of souls revisited the place, (valley of the Corf). Winter had brought back with it her annual visitors, untamed birds, despoilers of the crops. Such a flock of birds settled on the fields belonging to the virgin, ate the half-grown crops and ravaged everywhere. The loss is announced to the mistress, the mistress is not perturbed by the loss but as she was full of piety, was sorry for the loss. With power from her rewards and virtues she orders those wretched birds that none of them should remain in the fields. She threatens them in order that they might leave and that no loss befall the fields from this time forward, from them or from their descendants. What more? By the virgin's order the birds are pressed to depart, they are coerced by law not to harm her crops any more. A miracle happens, for those which had been untamed become domesticated to her instruction and obey her commands; they leave the fields. So thereafter they keep the orders of the mistress that whenever they come back each year at the return of the frost they repeat the miracle and they show an even more miraculous thing when, as if remembering her order and fearing to transgress her order, they avoid her fields and abstain from her crops. For either they flock down to pastures away from those, so as not to exceed their limits or, if tired of flying, they settle on them for just a little while (as if to get a breather) and then leave unfed quicker than you can say it. Oh how powerful is the merit of the virgin by which such a wonderful miracle is performed. What can be held indeed more sublime and remarkable than when something once shown is frequently repeated. This is repeated annually up to the present day and so testifies to itself by the annual repetition. When men of today see it they wonder at it and when they see it they rejoice and give glory to God'.

The third miracle story, telling how Milburga's veil was suspended from a sunbeam, has been claimed by other saints as well. Bridget of Kildare's 'rapt spirituality even caused her in her heedlessness of material things to hang her cloak on a sunbeam. (Milburn, 1961) Such stories were undoubtedly the accoutrements of the professional hagiographer. Goscelin included this particular story in Milburga's biography to highlight her piety and to illustrate her assiduity in prayer.

'Sometimes the holy virgin Milburga, equal to the angels, spent the night on divine matters. More awake than usual during the night she spreads herself with much delight among heavenly thoughts. Spending the night thus thinking of many things, she has pains in her body which is corrupted. She is wearied by earthly habitation, but finally goes to sleep about the end of the night. Dawn arises, night ends, the world is illumined by the sun. The sun lights up the virgin's bedroom, a place of prayer far more than of sleep. But in this change of light the virgin was not ashamed of a longer stay in her room since from it, by divine grace, shone forth an outstanding thing of an outstanding miracle. I shall speak of that wonderful thing. The sleeping virgin was struck by a ray of the sun that woke her from her dreams, and when awoken she is astonished, which happens to sleeping persons if they are aroused unexpectedly. While, as she usually did, she hurried to get up and prepared herself to go out early, in her astonishment as if by mistake she let her veil fall from her head. So that it did not fall to the ground, a ray of the sun, by divine approval, lifted it up and sustained it floating in the air near her until she came to her senses. The sun seemed to obey and venerate her with such a special miracle and to speak and to console her thus. "My lady, daughter of the most famous bride, light of the true sun, do not be angry with thyself, do not grieve anymore because you are so strangely awoken, struck by the ray of my sunbeam. Reflect and notice the indication of heavenly visitation which is clear to you through my angelic service. The angel is not revealed to you but it is your servant through me . . . I do not allow the flag of your sanctity and the standard of your angelic purity to touch the ground." Finally coming to herself the virgin of God recognised the heavenly miracle, she realised that she had been visited from on high and she poured out thanks to God and magnified him.'

The last of the four fully chronicled miracles is the story of Milburga's healing powers. Its likeness to Saint Matthew's account in the New Testament of Jesus healing the Cananite woman's daughter is possibly coincidental. (Mathew, chap. 15, verses 21–28). It is not for us to question the veracity of this and other miracles of healing attributed to Milburga during her lifetime and wrought by her relic later on. This story is as persuasive as a Biblical parable and serves to illumine her extraordinary spiritual strength and compassion.

'There was, it is said, a widow who was a neighbour of the blessed virgin Milburga. To her the love of her one surviving son was a solace to her widowhood and a sweet bond of the present life. It happened that he died and this inflicted a miserable wound on his mother. So his mother, surviving alone, not enduring the pain of her widowhood, did not know whither to turn while pain assailed her on every side. It was pain to see her one man dead and she did not want to be alive and separated from him. It was pain also to commit him to the grave when she would have preferred to be dead and to join him in his funeral. Bereft of child and husband she repeats her grief with tears and groans and she tortures and rends herself in many tearful ways. Finally, with hope against hope she believes to breathe again and she is divinely breathed on by the hope of the faithful Abraham, and transformed. The bereaved mother therefore collects her dead child and approached the aforementioned virgin of God, famed for her frequent virtues. Meeting her alone at her prayer time with God, she explained at her feet the wretched burden for the funeral, grieving and lamenting and shouting in her lamentation, – "wretched me, unhappy me, bereft of the comfort of my husband, destitute of the joy of my childbirth. What is more wretched than me, what more unfortunate? Alas, how I am distracted by manifest misfortune. Oh, happy friend of God, full of prodigous virtue, pity such an unfortunate woman such a desolate parent. Let him be restored, I beg you, let my dead son be restored to life through your prayer". This is what the anxious mother said to the virgin. What did the purest virgin reply? As she was the most compassionate consoler of all the afflicted she grieves and weeps with her. But because she had never yet experienced any such thing she is at a loss and denies what she is asked. She said to the mother, "It is not the wish of a sane mind what you so earnestly ask of me to be done. Go then and bury your dead son and prepare yourself for death in the future, after your son. For every man is born to this, that he should die. Death and destruction awaits each man and no-one is excepted". "I will not leave you", the mother says to the virgin, "unless you restore my child to me alive". Seeing therefore the vehemence of the grief of the bereaved mother, her determination and constancy of faith, the most kindly virgin of Christ is charged to undertake what she had feared to undertake. Forthwith prostrating herself in prayer by the dead body she held good that he who had been dead should live again. But before he returned to life something worthy of everlasting memory is said to have happened to the excellent virgin. For while she was prostrated in prayer by the dead son, a fire so great and so demonstrative came from heaven above her that she seems to be wholly consumed and burnt in it. Now, one of the nuns had concealed herself in the oratory for the sake of private prayer and saw what was happening. Not realising that the fire was divine and not understanding the mystical apparition, the woman thought that her mistress had been completely burnt up by such a fire. Fearfully she came nearer, investigating the affair and addressed the saint, shouting out repeatedly, "Mistress mine", she said "Mistress, arise quickly, get away out of doors, for I see you totally covered by a huge fire". This Mother Superior then saw the Virgin Milburga clinging to God with her whole mind, intent on heavenly things, fixed as if immoveable in prayer. And these women who had seen this wonderful vision were able to see even more wondrous things. Soon when Milburga's prayerful entreaties were accomplished the fiery appearance by which the nun thought that Milburga was being cremated, thinned out in front of her as she watched and stripped of the mystic fire the blessed virgin appeared neither hurt nor burnt. So

85

now, realising that the light which she had seen had been divine, the nun seriously upbraided herself because she had troubled Christ's divine bride with such terrible arias. Meanwhile when the holy incense had been lifted to the sky with groans and sighs for the dead man, and prayers and devotions had been poured out to God, the virgin with heavenly majesty and annointed with oil of heavenly happiness, arose from her prayer and lifted the dead man from the coffin. Restored to life, he is given back to his widow mother safe and well. And the mother, until now near death from grief, when she receives her son is resuscitated and is, as it were, snatched from the jaws of death. Then excited by joy she rushes into the public square and spreads the news of such a heavenly good deed. And there assembled into that one place the neighbouring crowd of holy people and clergy and singers and the praise of the virgin is raised up and glorified.'

The three Welsh miracles were written almost as an afterthought at the very end of The Life of Saint Milburga. Goscelin made it quite clear however that they are important enough to be included. They are all associated with Milburga's presence in Wales and it is possible that he travelled over the border to inquire of the Llanfillo folk more about the origin of the legends. On the other hand he may have relied on the monks at Wenlock and the English servants there or the oldest inhabitants of the village for information as he had done for the previous miracle stories. Goscelin was confident that 'the native people (the Welsh) worship these certain rites worthy of the memory of the virgin'. And he either saw for himself or heard first-hand about the three stones that marked the concrete evidence of the three miracles the last of which, erected near a church that could still be seen in his day.

'The virtues and miracles of the glorious virgin Milburga flourish still in Wales in a place which is called Llanfillo. In that place there lie three fairly large stones some distance apart from each other. One of them is said by the inhabitants to have been placed there in ancient times as a monument to divine vengeance. It was there that a certain pagan King of the Welsh was terribly smitten and fell down while pursuing the holy Milburga who he wanted violently to seize as his wife. The second (stone) retains in itself footprints impressed as it were in soft mud, by the mule of the virginal traveller. The natives venerate these imprints for their miraculous power and divine benefit. Rainwater collecting in those hollow footprints is collected and drunk by those with fever and in proportion to their faith their former health is restored. Likewise if water from the same source is poured on damaged eyes the grace of sight is restored to them by divine power. The third stone is said to have been the seat of the blessed virgin from whom it inhered such sanctity from her use of it that no beast could in any wise approach or feed on the grass which lay there without dying immediately or being seized by some terrible disorder. A house of prayer is erected there in honour of the virgin and as a sign of such holiness so that as if by divine law the approach of animals might be prevented. This stone is now surrounded by thorns so that what was formidable for beasts is now quite inaccessible. To the present day it is seen to lie before the doors of the Church as a heavenly warning to those who arrive that they should not enter God's House in a bestial way as not having intelligence and that they should not be miserably separated from Jesus Christ as the beasts seemed to be so divinely and miraculously warded off from that angular stone.'

Historical fact, legend and folk lore sound together throughout these tales, reminiscent of the primative counterpoint resounding in church music of the same date. To our modern ears they may seem quaint and unfathomable. Very little alteration has been made to the direct translation of the original text, only in places where the unravelling of sentences has been necessary to trace their obscure meaning. Goscelin's use of the present and past tenses has been held in place, mixed together, highlighting the urgency of the drama. The 'divine plan of salvation' embedded in each theme leads us through the puzzling series of events along the 'inscrutable course of the world' which is as mystifying today as it was in those centuries past.

XI

'I had a great and longing desire that God should give me deliverance from this life . . . I did not want to live and toil as it fell me to do . . . To all this our Lord in his courtesy gave an answer that brought comfort and patience. He said, "Suddenly you will be taken from all your pain, all your sickness, all your discomfort and all your woe." . . . In this word, "Suddenly you will be taken", I saw that God rewards man for his patience in waiting on God's will and God's time. Not to know the time of one's passing is a very good thing: if man knew it he would not wait patiently for it. All this living and waiting here is but a moment; when we are taken suddenly out of suffering into bliss, the suffering will be nothing.'   *Julian of Norwich*

' . . . and every day I look for the time when the Lord's rood, which once I gazed on here on earth, shall fetch me forth from this fleeting life and then shall bring me where there is great rejoicing, happiness in the heavens, where the Lord's people is seated at the feast, where there is bliss everlasting; and then He shall appoint me to a place where after I may dwell in glory, and fully share in joy among the blest.'

'Dream of the Rood', translated by M. Alexander

The exact date of Milburga's death is not known. The Oxford dictionary of saints puts it as early as 715, the Bollandist calculation gives it as 722 and Professor Finberg points out that 'charter proves that she survived into the episcopate of Bishop Wealhstod, 727–736'. ('Early English Charters of the West Midlands', p. 220.) Whatever the actual date of her death, it is certain that Milburga lived a long life, possibly into her sixties, at a time when the average life expectancy was about forty. She had escaped many of the common causes of death recently revealed by paleopathologists in their study of skeletal material from Anglo-Saxon cemetries; osteoarthritis of the spine from hard labour and damp conditions, death at childbirth and common hazards such as sword wounds, broken limbs and cuts. Goscelin is cautious about giving the exact number of her years when he writes, 'So far about sixty passages of years passed in the arena of transient passing life.' Writing about the death and burial of Saint Milburga, Angela Edwards states, 'It would indeed have been suspicious had Goscelin been able to furnish the date of St. Milburga's death. No means existed in the early eighth century Mercia for making such a computation. But there is no reason for refusing the evidence afforded for the day of her death, (the date of deposition) by early calendars. This day would immediately become memorable for the community of Wimnicas and would have been entered into whatever liturgical book the house possessed. From there it would have passed to other houses and into their calendars accordingly as the cult of St. Milburga developed. One may therefore with complete confidence, accept the evidence offered by three existing Pre-Conquest calendars, that St. Milburga died on the twenty third of February.' (Odo of Ostia's History of the Translation of Saint Milburga and its Connection with the Early History of Much Wenlock Abbey', p. 159).

Praises for Milburga's life and Christian example and her removal to Everlasting Glory became part of the Roman mass and liturgy celebrated in Latin at the churches belonging to her monastery. Saint worship in the eighth century was becoming part of the Christian tradition in England as it was on the Continent. This is most clearly seen in the Old English Martyrology, 'a book of potted lives of saints for reading aloud in monasteries.' (Mayr-Harting) It has been argued that the underlying conception of Saint worship belonged more to heathendom than to Christianity and that this custom, an old pagan idea, was managing to continue under the cloak of religion. 'The craving for local divinities in itself was heathen; in course of time the cult of the saints altogether re-moulded the Christianity of Christ. But the Church of Rome, far from opposing the multitude of those through whom the folk sought intercession with the Godhead, opened her arms wide to all.' (Eckenstein, 1896)

Goscelin's language becomes more and more elaborate as he describes the final days of Milburga's life and her departure to 'the lofty citadel of Joys'. She is borne aloft on a stream of florid sentences that must have left her faithful congregation wrapped in wonder as they listened to her final eulogy.

'... the kindly son of the Blessed Virgin Mary prepared for his bride the virgin, knocking on her door with the trouble of sickness as if inviting her to the marriage songs of heavenly marriage. She with weariness welcomed the prospect, the eminence of her holy old age being now advanced and replied to his knocking with every wish to enjoy fellowship with Him. For the more the pious mind of the virgin lay watchful for him with dawn's prophetic light, the more the flesh of the virgin thirsteth for him with prophetic ardour. So the angelic mother, daughter of the saints, rejoiced that there pressed on her the day for finishing her life on earth, on which she might cross over to that longed for day of eternal happiness. But so that the virginal light might be the more enflamed with burning desire to depart from the vale of tears to the lofty citadel of joys, her death is deferred for some time contrary to the prayer and hope of the virgin who so longed for it. For while what the wanter wanted is deferred, she sighed more for what she wanted. So this bride of Christ, avid for the heavenly bed-chamber, for the embrace of the eternal king, was assailed pressingly by disease of the body and there followed more keenly an onset of fevers. As the hurt to the body grew worse so the passing of the virgin was speeded up. She, tired by the fevers, is consecrated by heaven as a victim of our Lord; she loses breath and dies and she is wholly prepared for the heavenly bedchamber and made totally suitable for the divine embrace. Then what aromas of virtues did the heart of the sacred virgin breathe forth and give forth to the wanderings of the breezes. How pious were the flames of prayer blazing, how gentle were the balms of desire blazing from the inmost altar of her heart for the heavenly propitiation for the decease of true Solomon. How intimate her beseeching sighs so frequently penetrating heaven. How continuous her groans that fill the ears of heavenly piety. So the virgin Milburga, victim of God, consecrated as much by her martyr's mind as by desires for heaven reeked of heavenly aromas sweeter than all incenses. So happily she arranged the solemn day, amassing her virtues to present them to the majesty and glory of the altar on high. Here ends the life of the blessed virgin Milburga."

Milburga emerges as a shadowy figure from the legends supplementing the few historical facts we know. Under-standably her biographers who passed their information on to Goscelin were anxious to equate her life with earlier saints. The legends that grew around her name bear a great similarity to the Bible stories of healing and provision. Fact and legend became inextricably mixed and blurred the image of the woman who continued to lead her monastic community in their quest for spiritual excellence, long after her death. She became numbered among the saints whose lives were set apart from society in cenobitic monasticism; 'whose eyes were turned to the high stars, the very deep of Truth'. (Paulinus of Nola. 'To Ausonius'. – Waddell)

Another picture of Milburga comes more readily to view when the extent and wealth of her properties is appreci-ated. Della Hooke writes 'The success of the Much Wenlock foundation is shown by the way it gathered in such vast estates'. (Hooke) These have been described in full and in addition it is noteworthy to observe the strategic position of these properties and how they increased the power and defence of the Magonsaetan, the kingdom over which Milburga had such a great influence. Her Abbey at Much Wenlock was itself positioned close to the northern frontier, her lands at Lingen and the Monnow valley extended along the Welsh border, providing outposts long before Offa's Dyke was built as a defence. She acquired properties beyond the river Severn in the province of the Wreceon-Saetan and further to the south and east her monastery became landowner of Penda's Wrye in the heart of the Hwicce kingdom. It is not possible to draw any conclusions from the acquisition of these lands in neighbouring divisions of Mercia except to observe what must have been the far reaching influence of Milburga and her monastery.

Today's visitors to Much Wenlock Abbey cannot pay homage to the Anglo-Saxon princess abbess at a shrine or tomb and no epitaph records her saintly life. Only the walls of a much later monastery do her honour. These words written nine hundred years after Milburga's death by the scholar and preacher Thomas Adams, in 1631, explain the mystery of her reputation that shines out to us still from the 'Dark Ages'.

'It is a foolish dreame, to hope for immortalitie and a long-lasting name, by a monument of brasse or stone. It is not dead stones, but living men, that can redeeme thy good remembrance from oblivion. ... Onely thy noble and Christian life makes every mans heart thy Tombe, and turnes every tongue into a pen, to write thy deathlesse Epitaph.'   *Bush*

Epilogue

Description of a vision seen by a monk of the monastery at Wenlock

To the blessed virgin and best-loved lady, Eadburga, praise-worthy for her long perseverance in the observance of the monastic life, Winfred, one of the least in Christ Jesus, sends most affectionate greeting.

You have asked me, my dear sister, to describe to you in writing the marvelous visions of the man who recently died and came to life again in the convent of the Abbess Milburga, as they were revealed to him and were related to me by the venerable Abbess Hildelida. And now, thanks be to Almighty God, I am able to fulfill your wish more fully and more accurately because I myself spoke recently with the aforesaid resurrected brother when he returned to this country from beyond the seas. He then related to me in his own words the astounding visions which he saw in the spirit while he was out of the body.

He said that the extreme pain from a violent illness had suddenly freed his spirit from the burden of his body. He felt like a man seeing and wide-awake, whose eyes had been veiled by a dense covering and then suddenly the veil was lifted and everything made clear which had previously been invisible, veiled by a dense covering and then suddenly the veil was lifted and everything made clear which had previously been invisible, veiled, and unknown. So with him, when the veil of the flesh was cast aside the whole universe seemed to be brought together before his eyes so that he saw in one view all parts of the earth and all seas and peoples. And angels of such pure splendor bore him up as he came forth from the body that he could not bear to gaze upon them. With joyful and harmonious voices they sang:

'O Lord, rebuke me not in thy wrath; neither chasten me in thy hot displeasure.'

"They carried me up," he said, "high into the air, and I saw a mighty fire surrounding the whole earth, and flames of enormous size puffing up on high and embracing, as it were, in one ball the whole mechanism of the world, had not a holy angel checked it by the sign of the holy cross of Christ. For when the sign of the cross was made over against the threatening flame, it faded in great part and died away. I suffered intolerably from the heat, my eyes smarting and smitten by the glare of flashing spirits until an angel, splendid to look upon, laid his protecting hands upon my head and saved me from all injury by the flames."

He reported further that in the space of time while he was out of the body, a greater multitude of souls left their bodies and gathered in the place where he was than he had thought to form the whole race of mankind on earth. He said also that there was a crowd of evil spirits and a glorious choir of the higher angels. And he said that the wretched spirits and the holy angels had a violent dispute concerning the souls that had come forth from their bodies, the demons bringing charges against them and aggravating the burden of their sins, the angels lightening the burden and making excuses for them.

He heard all his own sins, which he had committed from his youth on and had failed to confess or had forgotten or had not recognized as sins, crying out against him, each in its own voice, and accusing him grievously. Each vice came forward as if in person, one saying: "'I am your greed, by which you have most often desired things unlawful and contrary to the commands of God." Another said: 'I am vainglory, by which you have boastfully put yourself forward among men." Another: "I am falsehood, whereby you have lied and sinned." Another: "I am the idle word you spoke in vain." Another: "I am sight, by which you have sinned by looking upon forbidden things." Another: "I am stubbornness and disobedience, whereby you have failed to obey your spiritual superiors." Another: "I am sluggishness and neglect in sacred studies." Another: "I am the wandering thought and useless notions in which you have indulged too much both in church and elsewhere." Another: "I am drowsiness, by which you were overcome so that you were late to make your confession to God." Another: "I am the idle errand."

96

Another: "I am negligence and carelessness, which have made you indifferent to the study of theology," and so forth.

Everything he had done in all the days of his life and had neglected to confess and many which he had not known to be sinful, all these were now shouted at him in terrifying words. In the same way the evil spirits, chiming in with the vices, accusing and bearing witness, naming the very times and places, brought proofs of his evil deeds. He saw there, also, a certain man upon whom he, while still numbered among the living, had inflicted a wound and who, he said, was still living, but now was brought in as a witness to his own misfortune. The bloody and open wound and even the blood itself cried out against him, charging him with the crime of bloodshed. And so, with his sins all piled up and reckoned out, those ancient enemies declared him guilty and unquestionably subject to their jurisdiction.

"On the other hand, " he said, "the poor little virtues which I had displayed unworthily and imperfectly spoke out in my defense." One said: 'I am obedience, which he has shown to his spiritual superiors.' And one: 'I am fasting, whereby he has chastened his body against carnal desire.; Another: 'I am the service of the weak, which he has shown by kindness to the sick.' Another: 'I am the psalm, which he chanted before God to atone for an idle word.' And so each virtue cried out for me in excuse for the corresponding sin. And those angelic spirits in their boundless love defended and supported me, while the virtues, greatly magnified as they were, seemed to me far greater and more excellent than could ever have been practiced by my own strength."

He reported further that he saw, as it were in the bowels of the earth, many fiery pits vomiting forth terrible flames and, as the foul flame arose, the souls of wretched men in the likeness of black birds sat upon the margin of the pits clinging there for a while wailing and howling and shrieking with human cries, mourning their past deeds and their present suffering; then they fell screaming back into the pits. And one of the angels said: "This brief respite shows that Almighty God will give to these souls in the judgment day relief from their punishment and rest eternal." But beneath these pits in the lowest depths, as it were in a lower hell, he heard a horrible, tremendous, and unspeakable groaning and weeping of souls in distress. And the angel said to him: "The murmuring and crying which you hear down there comes from those souls to which the loving kindness of the Lord shall never come, but an undying flame shall torture them forever."

He saw also a place of wondrous beauty, wherein a multitude of very handsome men were enjoying extraordinary happiness, and they invited him to come and share in their happiness if it were permitted to him. And a fragrance of wonderful sweetness came to him from the breath of the blessed souls rejoicing together. The holy angels told him that this was the famed Paradise of God.

He saw also a pitch-black fiery river, boiling and glowing, dreadful and hideous to look upon. Over the river a log was placed as a bridge. The holy and glorious souls, as they left their assembly, hastened thither, anxious to cross to the other side. Some went over steadily without faltering, but others, slipping from the log, fell into the infernal stream. Some of these were plunged in nearly over their heads, others only partly, some to the knees, some to the waist, and some to the armpits. And yet, each one of those who fell came up on the opposite bank far more brilliant and beautiful than when he fell into the foaming and pitchy river. And one of the blessed angels said of those fallen ones: "These are souls which after this mortal life with some trifling sins not quite removed, needed some kindly correction from a merciful God, that they might be a worthy offering to him."

Beyond the river he beheld shining walls of gleaming splendor, of amazing length and enormous height. And the holy angels said: "This is that sacred and famous city, the heavenly Jerusalem, where those holy souls live in joy forever." He said that those souls and the walls of that glorious city to which they were hastening after they had crossed the river, were of such dazzling brilliance that his eyes were utterly unable to look upon them.

He related also that there came to this assembly the soul of a certain man who had died while holding the office of abbot, a soul which seemed to be of rare beauty. The evil spirits seized upon it, claiming it as belonging with them. But one of the angel choir replied: "I will quickly show you, miserable spirits, that this soul is certainly not in your power." Thereupon a great troop of purified souls broke in and said: "This was our elder and our teacher, and through his instruction he won us all to God; at that price he was redeemed, and clearly he is not in your power." So they joined with the angels in their fight against the demons, and with the help of the angels they snatched that soul away from the power of the evil spirits and set it free. Then an angel spoke in reproachful words, saying: "Now then, know ye and understand, ye wretched spirits, that you captured this soul unfairly, so away with you into everlasting fire!" Now, when the angel had spoken thus, the evil spirits broke into weeping and howling, and in a moment, as in the twinkling of an eye, they hurled themselves into the pits of glowing fire described above; after a brief interval, emerging again, they began anew their arguments about the merits of souls.

The man related also that it was vouchsafed to him to look upon the merits of divers men still living. Those who were free from blame and who, trusting to their holy virtues, were known to have the favor of God Almighty were ever safely guarded by angels with whom they were joined in intimate affection. But those who were befouled with dreadful crimes and the stains of a corrupt life were closely beset by a hostile spirit, who ever urged them on to evil deeds, and as often as they sinned in word or act, he held them up to the merriment of other infernal spirits. When a man sinned, the evil spirit never waited for him to sin again but straightway called each desperate offense to the notice of the other spirits. On the instant he persuaded the man to sin, he immediately reported the sin to the demons.

Among other stories, he told how he had seen a girl of this world grinding grain. She saw lying near her a new distaff decorated with carving; she liked the looks of it and stole it. Then five of the most horrible spirits, filled with huge delight, reported the theft to their assembly and declared her guilty of theft. He said also: "I saw the sad soul of a certain brother who had died shortly before. I had ministered to him in his last sickness and had performed his funeral services. On his deathbed he bade me go to his brother, bear witness to his words, and, for the repose of his soul, ask him to set free a certain bondwoman who had belonged to them in common. But the brother, moved by avarice, did not comply with his request. And so this soul, in deep distress, was accusing his brother of breach of trust and was making loud complaints."

In the same way he bore witness concerning Ceolred, king of

Mercia, who, at the time these visions were seen, was unquestionably still alive. He said that he saw the king protected by a certain angelic screen against the assault of demons, as it were by a great open book held above him. But the demons begged the angels to withdraw the protection and permit them to work their cruel wills against him, charging him with a multitude of horrible crimes and threatening to have him shut in the deepest dungeons of hell, there to be racked with eternal torments as his sins deserved. Then the angels, more sadly than was their wont, spoke: "Alas! that this man of sin no longer permits himself to be protected, and that we can give him no help on account of his own demerits." So they withdrew the shelter of the protecting screen, and the demons with triumphant rejoicings gathered together from every part of the universe, in numbers greater than the narrator had supposed there were human beings living in the world, and tormented the king with indescribable cruelties.

Then, finally, the blessed angels directed the man who had seen and heard all these things in the spirit while he was set free from his body, to return into his body at once. He was not to hesitate to tell all that had been revealed to him to believers and to those who should question him with a pious purpose, but should refuse to talk to those who scoffed at him. He was to declare to a certain woman dwelling far away all her sins one by one and was to explain to her how she might give satisfaction to Almighty God if she were so inclined. He should declare all his spiritual visions to a certain priest named Begga and afterward proclaim them before men according to Begga's instructions. His own sins, which had been charged against him by impure spirits, he was to confess and expiate according to the judgment of that priest and, as directed by an angelic precept, he should confide to the priest that he had already for many years, for the love of God and without the knowledge of any man, worn an iron girdle about his loins.

He declared that his own body, while he was out of it, was so offensive to him that in all his visions he saw nothing so hateful and so contemptible, nothing except the demons and the glowing fires, that exhaled such a foul stench as his own body. Even his brethren, whom he saw kindly performing his funeral rites, he hated because they took such care of that odious body. However, by the angels' command, at daybreak he entered again into his body just as he had left it at cockcrow. After his return he was unable for a whole week to see anything whatever with his bodily eyes, filled as they were with bleeding tumors [*fisicis*]. Later he proved by their own statements that what had been declared to him by the angels concerning the pious priest and the sinful woman was true. And shortly afterward the death of the wicked king proved that what he had seen of him was the truth.

He reported also that he had seen many other similar visions which had slipped his memory, so that he could not recall the details, and he said that after those marvelous visions his memory was not as strong as it was before.

I have written down these things at your earnest request as he told them to me in the presence of three pious and most venerable brethren, who are known to be trustworthy witnesses and vouchers. Farewell, and may you live the life of angelic virginity, and reign forever with good report in heaven. Christ . . .

(The Letters of St. Boniface, translated by E. Emerton, *c.* (1940). Columbia University Press, New York, used by permission.)

Chronology

Relevant dates to Milburga's Life and Work

A. D.

630	Birth of Merewald.
638–690	Benedict Biscop.
644	Birth of Domneva.
654	Botulf began to build minster at Icanho – he had studied at Chelles.
654	Penda and his army with King Garynead and other allies from Wales march North.
655	Pendas's death at Winwaedfield killed by Oswiu of Northumbria.
655	Peada, Penda's son, succeeded to throne of Mercia, a complex of dependant kingdoms. Middle Angles – Hwicce – Magonsaetan – Lindsey
657	Peada's death.
657	Wulfhere succeeded the throne. Merewald's elder brother and married to Eormenhild, Domneva's cousin.
657	Merewald became King of Magonsaetan today the plain of Herefordshire north of the Wye, and South Shropshire.
660	Conversion of Merewald
661	Merewald married Domneva of Kent.
664	Birth of Milburga.
664	Synod of Whitby.
664	Year of pestilence.
666	Birth of Mildryth.
66(7)	Birth of Mildgith.
668	Appointment of Archbishop Theodore.

669	Birth of Merefin – only son of Domneva and Merewald who died in infancy.
671–3	Domneva returned to Kent, the murder of her two brothers, the founding of monastery at Thanet.
673–735	Bede.
674	Milburga, Mildryth and Mildgith sent to Chelles.
674	Wulfhere's death – killed by Oswiu's son, Ecgfrith. Ecgfrith became overlord of Mercia.
675	Seaxwulf became bishop of Mercia until 691.
675–754	Boniface.
678	Ethelred, Wulfhere's brother defeated Ecgfrith and Northumbria henceforward left the south alone – too occupied with their Northern borders.
680	Theodore created the dioscese of Hereford.
680	Death of Hilda of Whitby.
682	Milburga returned to the Magonsaetan from Chelles and possibly became novice at Much Wenlock under Liobsynde its founder and abbess.
684	St. Chad was appointed to the dioscese of Mercia.
685	The death of Merewald, buried at *Repton*.
685	Merchelm succeeded the kingship – son of Merewald not by Domneva.
685	Cuthbert became Bishop of Lindisfarne.
687	Milburga became Abbess of Wimnicas (Much Wenlock) and subsequently gave Liobsynde 60 hides at Hampton in exchange for Much Wenlock Abbey.
688	Tyrhtel was appointed Bishop of Hereford – until 710.
690	Death of Archbishop Theodore.
694	Withred succeeded to Kent throne – related to Milburga - great council held to consult about bettering of God's churches in Kent.
704	Coenred succeeded Merchelm.
706	Gulthlac's church at Crowland Abbey was dedicated, it belonged to the Mercian Royal house.
708–9	Welsh raids into Mercia.

709	Death of Aldhelm. Aldhelm dedicated his book in praise of virginity to Hildelith – Abbess of Barking who told Boniface about the 'Monks Vision' – so linked with Wimnicas.
709	Coenred left the throne to become a monk in Rome.
709	Coelred succeeded the kingship – he was dissolute.
710	Ecgwine became Bishop of Hereford. Both he and Milburga were in close touch with the Mercian court and he dedicated his church at Offenham to St. Milburga.
716	Death of Coelred.
716	Ethelbald succeeded the throne until 757. A great and powerful king. Built Watt's Dyke.
722–(727)	Death of Milburga. 23rd February her traditional feast day. The Madeley charter proves she survived into the episcopate of Wealhstod (727–736)

Bibliography

Alexander, M.(1986) – Translations of the earliest English poems. Harmondsworth: Penguin Books

Anglo-Saxon Chronicle (1961) – Edited by D. Whitelock *et al* London, Eyre & Spottiswoode

Bede (1849) – Ecclesiastical history of England. Ed. by J. A. Giles. 2nd ed. London: Bohn

Bede (1896) – Historiam ecclesiasticam gentis. Anglorum. . . ed. C. Plummer. Oxford University Press

Bede (reprint 1986) – A history of the English church and people. Trans. by L. Shirley-Price. Harmonsworth: Penguin Books

Benjamin, W. (1982) – Illuminations. London: Fontana

Beowulf (1970) – translated from the Anglo-Saxon by D. Wright. London. Panther

Boniface, *Saint* (1940) – Letters of . . . translated by E. Emerton. New York: Columbia University Press

Brontë, E. – Complete poems, edited from the manuscripts by C. W. Hatfield. Columbia University Press

Bush, D. (1952) – English literature in the earlier seventeenth century, 1600–1660. New York: Oxford University Press

Campbell, J. (1984) – The Anglo-Saxons. London: Phaidon

Cox, D. G. and Watson, M. D. (1987) *Journal of the British Archaeological Asssociation*. Vol. 140, pp. 76–87

Cranage, D. H. S. (1922) – The monastery of Saint Milburga at Much Wenlock. *Archaeologia* Vol. 72. p. 105

Croom, J. (1988) – The fragmentation of the Minster Parochiae in South East Shropshire. *In* Blair, J. *ed.* The local church in transition, 950–1200. Monograph, Oxford University Committee for Archaeology. No. 17

Crossley-Holland, K. and Gordon, R. K. (1978) – The Exeter Riddle Book. London, Folio Society

Dictionnarie d'Histoire et de Geographie Ecclesiastique (1953) Vol. 12. Paris, Letouzey et Ané

Eckenstein, L. E. (1896, reprinted 1963) – Women under monasticism: Chapters on Saint-Lore and convent life between A.D. 500 and A.D. 1500. Cambridge p. 15

Edwards, A. J. M. (1960) – Odo of Ostia's history of the translation of Saint Milburga and its connection with the early history of Much Wenlock Abbey. Thesis. London University Royal Holloway College

Edwards, D. L. (1981) – Christian England, London: Collins

Eyton, R. W. (1853) – Wenlock Priory. Archaeologia Vol. 5

Farmer, D. H. (1987) – The Oxford Dictionary of Saints. Oxford University Press

Fell, C. (1986) – Women in Anglo-Saxon England. Oxford: Blackwell

Finberg, H. P. R. (1961) – The Early Charters of the West Midlands. Leicester University Press

Finberg, H. P. R. (1972) – Anglo-Saxon England to 1042. In Finberg, H. P. R. ed. The Agrarian History of England and Wales. A.D. 43–1042. Cambridge University Press

Foster, F. E. A. (1899) – Studies in Church Dedication. London: Skeffington 3 vols.

Godfrey, C. J. (1962) – The Church in Anglo-Saxon England. Cambridge University Press

Goscelin – Vita Milburga. Additional Manuscript 34633 ff. 206–216. London: British Museum, (transl. by K. Workman)

Graham, R. (1939) – The history of the alien priory of Wenlock. Journal of the British Archaeological Association. 3rd series Vol. 4. p. 117

Hartshorne, C. H. (1841) – Salopia Antiqua. [London Library]

Herbert, G. – 'Man'. In: Oxford book of mystical verse (1924). Oxford University Press

Herman, N. (1989) – Too Long a Child: the Mother-daughter Dyad. London: Free Association Books

Hill, D. (1981) – An atlas of Anglo-Saxon England. Oxford: Blackwell

Hooke, D. (1986) – Anglo-Saxon territorial organisation: the western margins of Mercia. University of Birmingham, Department of Geography *Occasional Publication No 22*

Jackson, E. D. C. and Fletcher, E. (1965) – The pre-Conquest churches at Much Wenlock. *Journal of the Archaeological Association* 3rd. series. Vol. 28. pp. 16–38

Jackson, K. (1977) – A Celtic miscellany. Harmondsworth: Penguin Books p. 183

Jones, C. W. (1947) – Saints lives and chronicles. Ithaca, New York. Oxford University Press

Julian of Norwich (1980) – Revelations of divine love. Harmondsworth: Penguin Books

Levison, W. (1913) – Vita Bertia Abbatissae Calensis. *In*: Scriptores Rerum Merovingicorum vi. Hanover u. Leopzig

Levison, W. (1946) – England and the continent in the 8th century: Oxford University Press

Mayr-Harting, H. (1972) – The coming of Christianity to Anglo-Saxon England. London: Batsford

Milburn, R. L. P. (1961) – Saints and their emblems in English churches. Oxford. Blackwell

Noyes, A. (1910) – Collected poems. Vol. 2. Edinburgh: Blackwood

Owen-Crocker, G. R. (1986) – Dress in Anglo-Saxon England. Manchester University Press

Pretty, K. B. (1975) – The Welsh border and the Severn and Avon valleys in the 5th and 6th centuries A.D. an archaeological survey. Thesis. Cambridge University

Scott, A. F. *transl.* (1979) – Translation of The Ruin. *In*: Saxon age: Everyone a witness: commentaries of an era. London: Croom Helm

Shelley, P. B. – Hymn to intellectual beauty. *In*: Oxford Book of mystical verse (1924). Oxford University Press

Stenton, D. M. (1957) – English women in history. London. Allen & Unwin

Stenton, F. M. (1975) – Anglo-Saxon England. Oxford University Press

Tennyson, A. – The Holy Grail. *In*. The poetical works. London. Ward, Lock & Co.

Theophilus (1874) – Schedula diversarum artium... *Quoted in* Brown, G. B. (1903) The arts in early England. London. John Murray. p. 6

Waddell, H. (1952) – Medieval Latin Lyrics. Harmondsworth. Penguin Books

Webster, L. (1986) – Anglo-Saxon England A.D. 400–1100. *In*: Archaeology in Britain since 1945. Ed. by I. Longworth and J. Cherry. London. British Museum Publications

Whitelock, D. (1952) – The beginnings of English society. Harmondsworth. Penguin Books p. 149

Wilson, D. (1981) – The Anglo-Saxons. 3rd ed. Harmondsworth. Penguin Books

Woods, H. (1987) – *Journal of the British Archaeological Association* 3rd series. Vol. 140. pp. 36–75

Wordsworth, W. (1984) – Poems, ed. by Stephen Gill, Oxford University Press